Advances in Indigenous Dairy Products

Advances in Indigenous Dairy Products

Editor
Dr. Rajendra Kumar Pandey
Professor & Former Head
Department of Animal Husbandry & Dairying,
Institute of Agricultural Sciences,
Banaras Hindu University,
Varanasi – 221 005, U.P.
India

BIOTECH
2013
BIOTECH BOOKS®

ISBN 978-81-7622-264-8

Published by: **BIOTECH BOOKS®**
4762-63/23, Ansari Road, Darya Ganj,
New Delhi - 110 002
Phone: +91-011-23262132
E-mail: biotechbooks@yahoo.co.in

Printed at: **Chawla Offset Printers**
Delhi - 110 052

PRINTED IN INDIA

Preface

Milk production in Asia has expanded rapidly over the last three decades with annual milk production of 260 million tones in 2010. The milk production in India is growing at the rate of 4 per cent per annum as against the demand for milk consumption growing at the rate of 5-6 per cent. Therefore, the demand for milk and milk products continues to increase. Milk is considered a complete food. It has all the nutrients except iron. It provide more calcium and protein per monetary unit compared to any other food. Ratio of calcium and phosphorus in milk is very conducive for development and growth. Consumption of milk is also necessary for the growth of children.

Although, the traditional Indian dairy products enjoyed a great mass appeal because of their familiarities, understandings of the associated nutritional value and availability of good range of product categories at affordable prices, ironically limited processing technologies have been developed for commercial production of highly popular products like khoa, chhana, paneer, chakka and sweets derived there from. It may be of interest to mention that wide range of region specific traditional milk sweets of the different varieties, taste, and texture and huge utilized nearly 50 to 55 per cent of milk produced in India. The small scale techniques used in production lead to wide variations in chemical and microbiological qualities. Such methods needs to be upgraded and modernized enabling the dairy industry to adopt them for industrial application to match increasing demand in domestic and Global markets.

Many useful machines have been developed for batch and semi-continuous production of khoa, paneer, chhana, ghee and srikhand with some efforts for packaging and self-life extension. Such works need to be intensified. The facilities should be adequate and capable to convey technology, techniques, knowledge and information to the smallest and poorest. Otherwise the efforts made and results achieved by research and development would remain consigned to the laboratories. Integrated organization in basic to bringing dairy industry out as a vibrant and commercial structure that can benefit the poor, raise their status and reduce poverty.

This book is a sincere effort to extend the recent knowledge and developments in the field of Milk and milk products industry with special reference to the Indigenous Dairy Products with a view to familiarize these and explore the possibilities to adopt these technologies and develop the mechanization system for commercial production to popularize these products not only in India but into the Global Market

Dr. Rajendra Kumar Pandey

Contents

Chapter 1

By-Products from Ghee Industry and their Utilization

Chandrodaya Singh
Retired Professor and Head,
A.H. and Dairying
C.S.A. University of Agriculture and Technology,
Kanpur, U.P.

Since time immemorial, significant proportion of milk has been used for preparing a wide variety of traditional milk products *viz.* ghee, khoa, chhana, paneer, dahi, shrikhand, rabri and numerous dairy delicacies. These are the product of mass and are made because of their social, economic, religious, medicinal and cultural significance.

Ghee is one of the major indigenous milk products and accounts for 22 percent of the total milk production in India (Dairy India, 1977). The various by products obtained in different methods of ghee making are as under :

- ☆ Dedhi methods: Lassi (Butter milk) and ghee residue
- ☆ Creamery butter method: Skim milk, Butter milk and ghee residue
- ☆ Direct cream method: Skim milk and ghee residue

- ✰ Prestratification method and containuous method: Skim milk, butter milk (obtained during churning of butter melt in prestratification and ghee residue)

Thus three major by product are obtained from ghee industry namely :

1. Skim milk
2. Lassi or Butter milk
3. Ghee residue

Utilization of By-Products of Ghee Industry

Skim Milk

Flavoured Milk

There are milks prepared by skim milk to which flavours are added and its fat and S. N. F. percent is standardized to 2 per cent and 9 per cent respectively. If fat is less than 2 per cent they are called drinks. The main types are :

Chocolate Milk/Drinks

These contain 1–1.5 per cent cocoa-powder, 5–7 per cent sugar and 0.2 per cent sodium alginate stabilizer, milk is standardized after preheating to 35–40°C and filtering. After standardization again preheated to 60°C, homogenized at 2500 P. S. I. and then clarified. To the warm milk desired amounts of Cocoa mix, sugar and stabilizer are added slowly and stirred. The mixture is then pasteurized at 71°C for 30minutes, Cooled rapidly to 5°C, bottled and kept under refrigeration (5°) until used.

Fruit Flavoured Milk/Drinks

Permitted fruit flavours/essences, together with permitted matching colours and sugar are added. The method of preparation is similar to chocolate milk drinks. The common flavours used are strawberry, orange, lemon, pine apple, banana, vanilla etc.

Sterilized Flavoured Milk/Drinks

These combine the advantage of both sterilized and flavoured milk/drinks. Skim milk after receiving, cooled stored and preheated to 35–40°C. Then it is filtered/clarified and standardized and stored at 5°C till homogenization. At the time of homogenization, milk is preheated to 60°C and after homogenization filled in sterilized bottles after adding permitted flavours or essence and capped. Capped bottles are sterilized at 108–111°C for 25–30 minutes, cooled to room temperature and stored at this temperature till distribution.

Cultured Butter Milk

This is obtained by inoculation and incubation of pasteurized skim milk with lactic starter. Fresh skim milk is preferable. The solids content should range 9 to 10 percent. Manufacturing skim milk is heated at 82–88°C for 30 minutes. One percent bulk lactic starter is added after cooling to 22°C. after adding starter milk is not agitated until coagulation occurs and acidity between 0.80 to 0.85 percent is reached. Curd is broken up by agitation to give a smooth consistency and cooled to 5–10°C. It is then packed and stored at 5–10°C until distribution. Cream is added to impart rich flavour and decrease viscosity. Salt is added at 0.1 per cent to increase its flavour and butter granules or flakes are added to make it resembling butter milk.

Acidophilus Milk

In this product culture of *Lactobacillus bulgaricus* is used. It is claimed that acidophilus milk has therapeutic and health promoting properties. Its presence in intestinal tract checks putrefactive fermentations with a beneficial lactic fermentation.

Skim milk filtered/clarified at 35–40°C. After homogenization sterilized at 115°C for 15 minutes, cooled to 38–40°C, inoculated by 3–5 per cent culture, incubated at 38–40°C for 12–16 hours for coagulation. Coagulum is broken up and cooled to 10°C then packed and stored at 5°C until distribution.

Bulgarian Butter Milk

A pure single strain starter of lactobacillus bulgaricus is propagated for product manufacture. The incubation temperature range from 38 – 43°C. The finished product is characterized by higher acidity (1.2 – 1.5 percent).

Note: Skim milk can also used in the preparation of Srikhand, Dahi etc.

Lassi (Butter Milk Obtained by Churning Dahi)

Lassi is a refreshing beverage derived from churning of Dahi. It is popular drink of North India. Though certain versions of it are also consumed in other parts of the country. Aneja *et al.* (1989) Patented a processes for manufacture of long life Lassi. (Indian Patent No. 142362). This Lassi does not settle down over extended storage in aseptic packs.

Significant advancements have been made towards the industrial production of Lassi through application of U.H.T. standardized milk (9–10 per cent S. N. F. and 0.5–1.0 per cent milk fat) is fore warmed to 85°C for 30 minutes or 91°C for 2.5 to 5 minutes and cultured with suitable lactic culture (Dahi culture). It is then fermented at 22°C to lower the pH to 4.5 set curd is broken with the help of stirrer while sugar solution (30 per cent in water) is added so as to give 8–12 per cent sugar concentration in the blend. Lassi is then homogenized at 13.7 kpa (2000 P. S. I.) and U. H. T. processed at 135–145°C for 1–5 seconds and packaged aseptically employing standard equipments. A protocol for the mechanized production of Lassi is suggested in the following figure:

1000 Litre Milk in Multipurpose Vat

|

Standardization – 1.5 to 3.8% fat and 9% M. S. N. F.

|

Add 0.5 per cent sodium di-hydrogen phosphate

|

Pasteurization 90°C/15 minutes

|

Homogenization 150 kg/cm^2 (1st stage) and 50 kg/cm^2 2nd stage At 60°C and cool to 31°C

|

Culture addition (10 kg Lactic culture at 31°C)

|

Setting for 16 hour to pH 4.1

|

Breaking the firm curds by agitation for a min.

|

Add 0.5 per cent low methoxy pectin

Sugar 15 kg

|

Dissolving in water to make 25%s yrup

|

Straining

↓

Pasteurization

Addition of sugar syrup ← Sugar syrup

|

Addition of rose water/kewra flavour (20 ml) per litre Lassi

|

Homogenization/Passing through a pump

|

Mix well and let it stand for 1 hour

| U. H. T. treatment at 110°C for 4 second

Pouch filling ↓

(Non aseptic) Package aseptically

↓

Extended life Lassi

Butter Milk

Kadhi

To butter milk is added 5–8 per cent of Bengal gram flour (Beran) which acts as thickening agent. In addition boiled vegetables and fried balls (Pakora) of special Bengal gram (Besan) batter may be added at the end of preparation as filling materials. salt and sautéed onion along with spices may also be incorporated in kadhi. Kadhi exhibits typical cooked flavor and mildly acidic character.

Composition of kadhi varies from region to region depending on consumer preference. Milk solid content in kadhi; varies from 6 – 8 percent. To prepare instant version of kadhi, research work has been done to standardize a method for the manufacture of dehydrated kadhi a convenient product for making regular kadhi, dehydrated kadhi keeps well for 12 weeks when packed in low density poly ethylene pouches.

Rasogulla

Butter milk can also be used by mixing in pure milk upto 25 per cent for preparation of chhana and Rasogulla.

Ghee Residue

This is charred (burnt) light to dark brown residue obtained on the cloth strainer after the preparation of ghee. The composition of ghee residue varies depending upon the method of ghee making and method employed for the separation of ghee *i.e.* Hand or Mechanical. It contains heat denatured. Milk protein, caramelized lactose and varying amount of entrapped fat, besides some minerals and water. Thus, it is rich source of milk fat, proteins and minerals.

Utilization of Ghee residue

Direct Consumption

When made in small quantities it can be consumed as such with rice or chapati in producers household.

Preparation of candy and chocolate and use as a paste in sandwich spread and with Indian foods such as idli, dosa and samosa.

Before 'utilization excess fat is removed from the residue by enclosing the material in piece of muslin cloth and keeping the bundle suspended in a boiling water bath for 30–40 minutes. The bundle is then taken out and the water allowed to drain out first by it self and then gently squeezed when partially cool. After this, the residues are given a pretreatment by boiling in a similar manner in 10 per cent sodium bicarbonate solution, which should be constantly stirred during cooking. The processed cooked ghee residues can be made into Candy and Chocolate as under :

Candy

A 50 per cent sugar syrup is first prepared the cooked residue is thoroughly mixed into the syrup in a karahi by means of a khunti. The mixture is heated on a low fire until sufficient water is evaporated. To this sticky mass powdered dry coconut may be added and candy evenly spread on a plate (5–10°C) for an hour to allow it to cool. It is then cut into small cubes and wrapped in parchment paper for storage at room temperature till marketed. For every 1 kg cooked residue 500–625 g sugar and 125–250 g coconut powder is required.

Chocolate

Cooked residues are mixed with 50 per cent sugar syrup as above. To sticky mass cocoa power and skim milk powder are added and stirred vigorously till a pat is formed. Finished product is spread on plate and allowed to cool (5–10°C) for an hour. It is then cut into small cubes and wrapped in parchment paper for storage at room temperature till marketed. For every kg cooked residue 500–625g sugar, 60 – 90g cocoa powder and 250g skim milk powder is required.

Paste

Cooked residue is mixed with salt @ 2.5–3 per cent, then with marmite (a yeast product) @ 0.1–0.5 per cent, heated on low fire for about 5 minutes till a paste is formed. This can be used in sandwiches. Alternatively, the salted residue is mixed with chutney power @ 2–4 per cent, ground thoroughly and then heated as above to yield a paste for use with idli, dosa and samosa.

Burfi Type Sweet (Chocsidu Burfi)

The processed sweet ghee residue is mixed with standard quality khoa (prepared using 5 per cent fat standardized buffalo milk and khoa with 30 per cent moisture) in proportion of 1 : 1 of solids content. This mixture is heated in steam jacketed kettle and thoroughly agitated with a khunti to ensure proper mixing. All the crystal sugar @ 45 per cent of total solids in khoa and 75 per cent of the total solids in the processed residue is now added to the mixture, which is then worked rigorously for 10–15 minutes to dissolve the sugar completely. One third of the sweetened mass is separated and mixed with chocolate @ 8 per cent of the total solids content of the processed residue khoa and well mixed into it. This portion containing chocolate is applied as a thin layer over the remaining two thirds of mixture which has already been spread out as a thick layer on a well greezed tray. Whole mass cooled, cut into pieces and packed for sale.

Chapter 2

Quality Control in Indian Milk Products Manufacture and Introduction of Management Systems Therefore

Chandrodaya Singh

Rtd. Professor and Head

A.H. and Dairying,

C.S.A. University of Agriculture and Technology,

Kanpur, U.P.

Indian has made great stride in milk production and presently ranks first in the world. Quality milk production will be a major challenge for the 21st century. It is to be viewed in the back drop of deteriorating milk quality standards in the country. We have achieved tremendous improvement in milk production but the quality aspect have been most neglected, leading to poor quality milk and milk products. Moreover, we are to face a more open and liberal market both domestic and abroad. With this changing scenario, we have to gear our selves to wards better quality of milk to meet the demands of the market.

Cross breeding programme and changes in feeding pattern of milch animals, the milk of some animals does not meet the legal PFA standards. This has resulted in the adulteration of milk even with harmful substances to raise requirements. In the recent past, due to liberalization policy of Government of India, there is tremendous mushrooming of dairy plants which has resulted in scarcity of natural milks especially during summer season. The milk procurement also starts dealing during the lean season. This is the period when un scrupulous lements try to harvest the gain by adulterating the natural milk using all type of pond water, salt sugar, wheat flour, baking soda, washing soda, caustic soda, urea, hydrogen peroxide, formaline and different vegetable oil and animal body fat have been known to be in use depending on need and situation. Some of the adulterants are used for increasing the volume of milk, while others are used for preserving and extending the shelf life and to meet the legal standards of milk. The phenomenon of adulteration goes on changing in terms of ingredients to make maximum profit. In November 1994 reports appeared in different news papers and magazines indicating that in several parts of the country the milk vendors are selling synthetic milk which is prepared using harmful chemicals. The term synthetic milk is misnomer and is probably coined by the media person for adulterated milk. From synthetic milk one would normally under stand a product analogous to natural milk in its physical, chemical and nutritional properties. But there is no similarity between the two. Who can synthesize milk other than milch animals? Synthetic milk is gross misuse of knowledge of chemistry *i.e.* process of saponification. The basic ingredients used in the manufacture of synthetic milk are caustic soda, water, refined vegetable oils, animal body fats, urea, detergents, sugar, salt and skim milk powder. Detergents increase viscosity of the solution and vegetable oil prevent frothing in the solution. Soap sopanifies the oil into an emulsion which liberates free fatty acids into the milk.

Adjustment of non fat solids in milk is done and acidity is neutralized by using caustic soda. Lactometer is used to adjust specific gravity of synthetic milk equal to that of natural milk.

In the past WTO regime of liberalized trade, regulatory aspects of food standards are crucial to words consolidating the benefits of new free trade agreement. Dairy industry will be able to amass possible benefit by being a global contender in trade only after its products are at par with those of the rest of world. The Indian food industry will sustain only if it is able to provide a competitive edge vis-a-vis price and quality.

Quality

Quality has been defined as "The totality of characteristics of an entity that bears on its ability to satisfy stated and implied needs". The importance of quality can best be explained in the words of sueo yamaguchi, consultant. J I P M "Quality is not some thing to be discussed in Japan; it is not some thing you talk about. It should be there, that's all that is how it should be in India too".

There was a time when people used to stand in long queues to get their daily quota of milk. Quality was not critical. Today the scene is different; no one sees long queues at milk booths. If customers are not happy with supplier, they go to another. Dairies have understood that quality products and services are the key factors for winning over customer.

Emphasis On Quality Control

Strict system of quality control is needed in order to provide consumers milk and milk products with high quality. The system begins with production and procurement of milk. Milk should be tested at the processing centre for fat, S.N.F., acidity, bacteriological quality and presence of preservatives or neutralizers which are not permitted by law. After processing the milk should again be checked for bacteriological staying qualities, as well as fat and S. N. F. content in order to ensure that it meets the rigid standards. Spot checks should also be made at retail out let's to ensure that the required quality standards are met. Besides product control strict control should be kept on sanitation, both at the plant and retail out lets. Besides chemical and bacteriological tests for products, processing equipment should also be subjected to regular bacteriological tests. Water in dairy should be softened, chlorinated and regularly tested to maintain highest standards. Quality of water used at booths and insulated containers should also be checked.

International and Indian Standards For Dairy Products

To keep pace with newer scientific and technological developments, the revision of standards has been entrusted to the Codex Committee on Milk and Milk Products (CCMMP), established in 1993. During its several deliberations, 11 standards have been revised and adopted by the CAC. Owing to interventions by the Indian delegation, certain alterations have been made in some standards. A few pertain to the definition of milk, inclusion of ghee in the standard Milk Fat Product, incorporation of BHA as an antioxidant and removing the restriction of permitting only cow milk as a raw material, particularly for cheese. Due to continued efforts by India at the IDF as well as CCMMP, a scientific proposal illustrating the suitability of buffalo milk for cheese making was prepared, thus relaxing the earlier restriction.

There are certain areas where discrepancies still exist in Indian and international standards. In India, a level of 0.2 ppm of lead in milk is considered safe, whereas international requirements are fixed at 0.02 ppm. The level of lead in butter (maximum of 0.05 mg/kg) was not acceptable to the Indian delegation, but was adopted by the CAC as it had been already endorsed by the Codex Committee on Food Additives and Contaminants (CCFAC). Differences between existing Codex and PFA standards of pesticide residues in milk have been documented by Varshney (2000). The differences in some of the quality standards for ghee are also listed. There are CAC guidelines for the use of lactoperoxidase system for the preservation of milk, but the LP – system is not permitted in India. Similarly, using decolorized buffalo milk is permitted in several nations, but not India.

International Standards on Quality and Food Safety Management Systems

World is witnessing technological breakthroughs and emerging global markets. Global standardization and certification systems encapsulate these developments and provide tools to facilitate international transactions of goods and services. Thus standardization and quality systems have become sin – qua – non for development of the national economy all over the world. It is in this context that ISO 9000 quality management systems standards brought out by International Organization for Standardization (ISO) and Food Safety Management Systems (HACCP) standards brought out by the Codex Alimentarius Commission (CAC) have assumed greater importance for achieving the objective of facilitating global trade for safe and whole some foods.

Table 2.1: ISO Standards on Quality Systems

ISO No.	*Title*
ISO 8402 : 1994	Quality management and quality assurance – vocabulary
ISO 9000 – 1 : 1994	Quality management and quality assurance standards – Part 1 : Guidelines for selection and use.
ISO 9000 – 2 : 1997	Quality management and quality assurance standards – Part 2 : Generic guidelines for the application of ISO 9001, ISO 9002 and ISO 9003 (first revision of ISO 9000 – 2 : 1993).
ISO 9000 – 3 : 1997	Quality management and quality assurance standards – Part 3 : Guidelines for the application of ISO 9001 to the development, supply and maintenance of software (first revision of ISO 9000 – 3 : 1991)
ISO 9000 – 4 1993	Quality management and quality assurance standards – Part 4 : Guide to dependability to programme management
ISO 9001 : 1994	Quality Systems – Model for quality assurance in design/ development, production, installation and servicing.
ISO 9002 : 1994	Quality systems – Model for quality assurance in production, installation and servicing
ISO 9003 : 1994	Quality systems – Model for quality assurance in final inspection and test
ISO 9004 : 1 : 1994	Quality management and quality system elements – Part 1 : Guidelines
ISO 9004 – 3 : 1991	Quality management and quality system elements – Part 2 : Guidelines for services
ISO 9004 – 3 : 1993	Quality management and quality system elements – Part 3 : Guidelines for processed materials
ISO 9004 – 4 : 1993	Quality management and quality system elements – Part 4 : Guidelines for quality improvement
ISO 10005 : 1995	Quality management – Guidelines for quality plans
ISO 10006 : 1997	Quality management – Guidelines for quality in project management
ISO 10007 : 1995	Quality management – Configuration management
ISO 10011 – 1 : 1990	Guidelines for auditing quality systems – Part 1 : Auditing
ISO 10011 – 2 : 1991	Guidelines for auditing quality systems – Part 2 : Qualification criteria for quality systems auditors
ISO 10011 – 3 : 1991	Guidelines for auditing quality systems – Part 3 : Management of audit programmes

Contd...

Table 2.1–Contd...

ISO No.	*Title*
ISO 10012 – 1 : 1992	Quality assurance requirements for measuring equipment – Part 1 : Meterological confirmation system for measuring equipment
ISO 10012 – 2 : 1997	Quality assurance requirements for measuring equipment – Part 2 : Guidelines for control of measurement processes
ISO 10013 : 1995	Guidelines for developing quality manual
Hand Book	ISO 9000 Handbook for small business – What to do – Advice from ISO/TC 176

Quality quest – Volume 9 No. 3, July 2000, p. 27.

HACCP for Quality Management in Dairy Trade

Hazard analysis and critical control point the international food handling safety standards ensure cleanliness, hygiene and sanitation in handling milk and milk product and give an assurance of safety to consumers. Indian is signatory to WTO agreement and have understood its significance and started the process of educating the farmers to produce clean milk at village level, handle it hygienically and transport it quickly or in cool condition to dairies for processing it further in to milk and milk products. The HACCP plays a major role in clean milk production. It provides:

1. A proactive system for assuring safe production and delivery of foods.
2. Emphasis on prevention rather than inspection.
3. A system of addressal for all types or hazards – microbiological, physical and chemical.
4. Scope for integration into more general quality assurance plan.
5. International acceptance.

In short it is about food safety management. A vital feature in the entire chain of milk management from the farm to the consumers. Mother dairy was the first to be certified for HACCP (I S : 1500) by the Bureu of Indian standards.

International Agreements Facilitating Dairy Trade

The trade reforms initiated by the world trade organization (WTO) have already changed the business environment. The Technical Barriers to Trade (TBT) and sanitary and phyto sanitary (SPS) agreements have been brought under WTO to facilitate and mitigate obstacle to international trade. These agreements envisage application of international standards, international certification systems and bringing transparency in the-promulganation of national regulatory requirements as means of facilitating international trade of food. SPS is particularly applicable to food industry and adoption of HACCP standard under the agreement makes it mandatory for the food industry to apply food safety management systems for facilitating international trade.

TBT

It covers all the types of standards including aspect of food standards (except requirements related to sanitary and phytosanitary measure) and include large number of measures designed to protect the consumer against deception and economic fraud. Food standards it covers relate to quality requirements, labeling and methods of analysis. The agreement provides all the technical standards and regulation must have a legitimate propose and that the impact or cost of implementing the standard must be proportional to the trade. It should also facilitate trade. Under this agreement, each country has to operate an enquiry point, which is able to answer all reasonable enquiries from member countries and interested parties on technical regulations, standards and conformity assessment systems.

Sanitary and Phyto Sanitary Agreement (SPS)

The SPS agreement requires that member countries base their national measure on international standard, guideline and other recommendation adopted by codex Alimertarius commission, a joint FAO and WHO commission, where they exist. As lodex standards have the full support of SPS agreement which advocates them as basis for all national standards, they will play a significant role in harmonization of national food safety standards with increasing international trade in food stuffs and specific requirement of SPS agreement there is a need for uniform guideline for inspection and certification systems in all countries. The SPS agreement requires that inspection and certification system should ensure transparency, equivalency and risk based systems.

Integration of ISO 9000 and HACCP

ISO 9000 encompasses all the activities of a dairy to ensure that it meets its quality objectives and HACCP system is directed towards ensuring safety of food. ISO 9000 and HACCP, one concerned with quality and another for food safety management systems respectively, have much in common. In fact quality in broader sense includes food safety.

Conclusion

Consumer trades are changing. Technological advances are taking place. Organic dairying is the emerging slogan. At this junction consumer satisfaction is the key force that will determine the future strategies with regard to quality and safety of food.

Chapter 3

Emerging Trends in Manufacture of Traditional Dairy Products

B.R. Ulmek
Head
Department of Animal Science and Dairy Science
M.P.K.V., Rahuri, Ahmednagar – 413 722

Since time immemorial a significant proportion of milk has been used in India for preparing a wide variety dairy delicious. These traditional dairy products have played a significant role in the economic, social, religious and nutritional well being. It is estimated that 50 to 55 per cent of milk (approx. 42MT) is converted by traditional sector *i.e.*, Halwais into traditional dairy products, using process such as heat and acid coagulation, heat desiccation and fermentation (Banerjee, 1997). The market for Indian milk products is estimated to be of the order of Rs 578 billion (Aneja *et al.*, 2002). This fact underlines the significance of traditional dairy products in the national economy.

In spit of such a great importance of traditional dairy products in our country, these products are still produced manually in the small sector with variable quality products are still produced manually in the small sector with variable quality depending on the skill of halwais. There is hardly any quality control and the shelf life is poor. The rural scale operations are associated with inefficient use of energy, poor hygiene and sanitation and non-uniform product quality. Most of the preparations are labour intensive and relay on local inputs. The marketing of these products by halwais (most sale during festival) and very less attention is paid to packaging and sanitary handling practices.

Increasing demand of these product present a great opportunity for the organize dairies in the country to modernize and scale up the production. Therefore, the expanding business prospects provided by these products call for a reconstruct this sector.

Large-scale manufacture of these products in a hygienically safe manner, with assured quality control and proper packaging will certainly do wonders for this sector not only in India but also in abroad. Lead has initially been taken in this regard by NDDB's dairy like Sugam, Sabar, Rajokel, Warna, etc (Patil, 2002). There is need to look into our strength, Weaknesses, opportunities and threats and accordingly re-evaluate and re-engineer as to modernize traditional dairy product sector (Table 3.1).

Table 3.1: SWOT Analysis of Traditional Dairy Product Sector

Strength
Traditional dairy products enjoy mass appeal.
Simple manufacturing technologies.
Skilled manpower for cottage scale operations available.
Lower cost of production and high profit margins.
Niche markets are well established.
Require low infrastructure and operational overhead cost.
An optimistic demand profile-consumption likely to grow 20 per cent/annum.
Permit significant value addition, unparalleled by other dairy products.
Weaknesses
Lack of scientifically documented.
Manufacturing operations are predominantly confined to thecottage/domestic scales.
Halwais lack adequate knowledge of good hygienic practices.
Gross lack of packaging systems that severely limit of shelf life.
Lick of quality/legal standards and quality assurance systems
Regional specificity of traditional dairy products.
Lack of production statistics based on realistic surveys.

Contd...

Table 3.1–Contd...

Opportunities
TDP sector offers vast scope for innovation, value addition and productdiversification.
Grater demand due to higher purchasing power of the newly emerging middle class.
Greater access to global market under WTO regimen.
Export potential to the ethnic markets.
Threats
Products prepared by scaled-up processes/new equipments may differ insensory quality and may not find consumers acceptance.
Modern methods of manufacture may raise production cost.

Classification of Traditional Dairy Products

The varieties of traditional dairy products are produced in India, most of which are region specific.

Process	*Base Product*	*Milk Product/Sweet Obtained from to Base Product*
Heat desiccation	Khoa	Burfi, Kalakand, Peda, Milk, cake, Gujja, Gulamjamun, Lalmohan, Kunda/ doodh pak.
Concentration	Rari, Khurchan Malai, Basundi	Rosogolla, Sandesh, Rasmalai, Chumchum, Channamurki, Kirmohan, Seetabhog, Rajbhog, Chhana Kheer
	Paneer	Panner tikka, Paneer samosa, Paneer-e-Kofta, Paneer pakora, Paneer-e-Pasand, Panner Kheer.
	Bandel Cheese, Durukho, Surti Panner	
	Sherghum	Shoshim
	Kachha churpi	Dudh churpi
	Dahi	Lassi, Chhach, Kadhi, raita, Chakka, Shrikhand, Shrikhand wadi
	Masti dohi	

Contd...

Table–Contd...

Process	*Base Product*	*Milk Product/Sweet Obtained from to Base Product*
Fermentation	Makhan/Loni	Ghee
Freezing	Kulfi, Kulfa, malai-ka burf	–
Concentration	Gereal-based	Kheer, Halu Kheeru (Rice) Payasam
of milk-cereal/	Pulse-based	Kadele ble, Paysam
public mixture	Tuber cropbased	Kaddu-ki-Kheer, Sabbakki
	Fruit based	Halorina, Mavina, Payasam
	Seed based	Khus Khus, Payasam

An Optimistic Demand Profile

Product	*Current Demand 1998 (MT)*	*Project Demand 2009 (MT)*
Ghee	1,00,000	2,00,000
Cheese	4,100	15,000
Paneer	1,000	16,000
Shrikhand	3,000	5,650
Rosogolla	1,600	6,000
Gulabjamun	3,000	5,850
Yoghurt	375	800

Source: GCMMF-TCS survey report.

Mechanization of Manufacture of TDP

In order to overcome the inherent disadvantage associate with conventional method of manufactures of TDP such as

Disadvantages of Traditional Method

- ✩ In efficient use of energy
- ✩ Poor hygiene and sanitation – as it open to environment
- ✩ Non-uniform product quality-chemical, microbial and sensory
- ✩ Poor packaging

- Excessive strain and fatigue on the operator
- Limited shelf life (Dharam Pal, 2000)

Attempts have been made to develop batch semi continuous equipment for the manufacture of these products.

Need of Modernization

- Disadvantages with traditional method.
- Demand/population increases.
- Improved purchasing capacity
- TDP enable the dairy plants to become economical viable and also sustain fluid milk
- Export potential

Network Project

A network project finance by ICAR for modernization of technologies for a few TDP has been operated since 8th five year plan with Karnal as the main center and three centers located at Anand, Banglore and Mohanpur.

Technology Used in Manufacture

The types of traditional technologies which being adopted since long time and improved with the passage of time are summarized are in Table. A range of product is very widely accepted for direct consumption or their different application.

Technology Used in Manufacture

Sl.No.	Indigenous Dairy Product	Technology Used
1.	Coagulated Product Channa and Paneer	Acid Precipitation Thermal concentration Flirtation Coagulum processing
2.	Fermented Cultured products Dahi, Lassi, Misti-dahi	Thermal concentration Cooling Culture Addition Incubation Processing

Contd...

Table–Contd...

Sl.No.	*Indigenous Dairy Product*	*Technology Used*
3.	Fat-rich Products Butter and Ghee	Skimming Churning Thermal Concentration Filtration
4.	Concentrate productivity Koha	Thermal concentration

Source: Nanda and Sexena (2000).

Mechanization of Desiccated Milk Based Product

Khoa

- ☆ Khoa is obtained by rapid drying of milk
- ☆ Contain not less than 20 per cent fat of finished product.
- ☆ Size of industry

  Production: More than one million tones

  Milk utilized: 6million tones (7 per cent fat)

  Confined: Non-organized sector mostly

  Mechanized plant: More than 20

Inclined SSHE Khoa-Making Commercial Plant at Sugam Dairy, Vadodara (Dr. J.S. Punjrath, *et al.*, 1990)

In this machine, concentrate milk of 42 to 45 percent TS is used as feed. The inclined design of the heat exchanger permits the formation of pool of boiling milk which constantly moves forward and get applied on the heat surfaces as a thin film by the scrapper agitator on the heating surface concentrates milk is coagulated to form semi solid khoa.

The schematic continuous K. system developed by Dodja et al. (1992). In this, two SSHE, were arranged in cascade fashion. The rotor of first SSHE was provided with four variavle clearance blades and operated at 3.3 RPS. Milk was concentrates in it in the range of 10-45 per cent TS. This concentrated product from first SSHE entered the second SSHE, which had a different kind of rotor arrangement. It had two variavle clearance blades and two helical bladders. Further, it was operated a at a lower speed of 2.5 RPS.

New technology for industrial production of Gulabjamun has been developed using as lassembly- line system and is in operation at the sugam unit of Varoda Dairy. Canned Guabjamune is now veing largely exported to the Gulf countries and America. Several dairy plants in India and avroad are producing gulabjamun on a large scale.

Peda

- ☆ Popular all over India
- ☆ Production exceeds than any other TDP
- ☆ Prepared by mixing khoa and sugar (3:1)
- ☆ Recently, some plants have under taken peda producing using mechanized equipment and Rheon extruder.
- ☆ They use the planetary mixer for affecting uniformity from batch to batch.
- ☆ The R&D Group o NDDB Anand, has recently developed a peda-moulding machine and continuous peda line.

Burfi

1. Improve flavour and texture of khoa and there by adaptability.
2. Varieties: Plain, mawa, pasta, nut, chocolate, coconut and Rava burfi.

Industrial Manufacture

Champak(1998) carried out investigation at NDRI Karanl, on manufacture of burfi of acceptable quality, a thin film scraped surface heat exchanger (ISSHE) can be utilized for initial concentration of milk. Cardamom and potassium sorbet are added @ 0.1 per cent of khoa (W/W) as a preservatives followed by hot packaging of the product into multiplayer co-extruded nylon barrier pouches under vacuum. This method permitted as shelf life of about 45 days at 30°C.

A mechanized process for commercial production of burfi was successfully developed by NDDB and installed at Sugam Dairy.

Mechanized Process for Production of Burfi at Sugam Dairy, Vadodara

In this process for production of the plain burfi, all the ingredient *viz.*, khoa, sugar and additives, such as cardamom nuts etc. are first heat processes to blend uniformly in a planetary mixer. The processor ingredients are then fed to a Rheon shaping and forming machine. You may impart the size and shape on own occurs. Burfi is then packed in corrugated cardboard boxes film having structure PE/ bonded layers and nylon/bounded layer have also been successfully tried.

Heat-Acid Coagulated Products

1. Channa and paneer are two prominent traditional coagulated milk products of the India sub continuous, Verma (1998).
2. The practice of curdling of milk to prepare certain milk products was popular in ancient India.

Channa: Used for the preparation of a large variety of India delicious namely, rasogolla, sandesh, cham cham, vasammol, pantoog, rajbhog.

Production site: Eastern Region and Bikaner (RJ)

Production: 2000,000 tonnes

Value of channa sweets: Rs.70000 million

Aneja (1977) developed a prototype continuous channa-making machine with a capacity of 40 kg channa/hr. at NDRI Karnal. The major components of the equipment are in Fig.8. In the prototype the milk is pumped to a tubular heat exchanger, where it is heated to a temperature of 90 to 95° C. There after, The milk comes in contact with sour whey of desired acidity. The mixed milk and whey is then pumped and circulated through holding coils for its complete coagulum and cooling. The length of holding coil ensure the minimize residence time for coagulum. Ultimately the, product is brought into a cechanical strainer where it is drained to a desired level. The product will be of inferior quality in case the excess moisture is not drained to a desired level.

Paneer

☆ Obtained by acid coagulation.

- ☆ Topically, paneer is marble shite in appearance
- ☆ Having a slightly spongy body, close knot texture
- ☆ Possessing a sweetish acidic nulty flavours.
- ☆ Milk fat content shall not be less than 50 per cent of DM.

Size of Industry

- ☆ Confined to the non-organized sector
- ☆ One percent milk production is converted to panner
- ☆ Annual production is estimated 150,000 tonnes.
- ☆ The cost of production is lower
- ☆ The yield range from 17 to 18 per cent
- ☆ One private plant (U.P.) handle 25000 litre milk per day

Industrial Process

Mathur *et al.* (1993) developed the continuous process which involve the pasteurization of standardized milk(1.5 per cent fat and 9.5 per cent SNF) followed by ultra filtration to a TS content of 30 per cent To this gluconod-lactose is added @ 0.9 per cent prior to filling in reportable moralized polyester pouches of 200 or 500 ml. These sachets are then sterilized in an autoclave at 110°C for 14 minutes during which concomitant thermal texturization also takes place resulting in formation of a long shelf life product. Schematic drawing of assembley line production of paneer also described.

Masti Doi

- ☆ Also called payo dahi and lal dahi
- ☆ Well established dessert in the eastern part
- ☆ Continued to domestic cottage scale production
- ☆ However, standardized Mashti Doi is now being marketed in metro cities.

Product Description

- ☆ Fermented milk productivity
- ☆ Creamish to light brown colour
- ☆ Firm consistency, smooth texture and pleasant aroma
- ☆ Sugar contains 17 to 18 per cent
- ☆ Total solid contains 32-36 per cent

Technology

Aneja (2002) described the procedure for masti doi preparation.

- ✰ Milk and cream in required proportion are mixed in multipurpose vat.
- ✰ SMP added to increase total solid continue caramel is added @ 0.1 to 0.12 per cent before starting the heating of the mix. (If caramel is added to mix above 50°C, undesirable flakes would be formed.
- ✰ The mixture heated to plate pasteurized to 80-90°C
- ✰ It has been observed that heating the mix to 85°C and holding for 15 minutes yield a product of desirable quality and texture.
- ✰ Cool to 40-45° C temperature by circulating water in the multipurpose vat.
- ✰ Add 1 per cent culture at 43° C temperature of mixture after that the masti Doi mix as filled in sanitized caps. The temperature should be around 41° C.
- ✰ Lids are heat sealed on caps to make them air tight and prevent leakage of the mixture. The sealed cap are then placed in trays/crates.
- ✰ The cups are incubated at 41° C temperature for about 6 to 8 hr. till acidity develop to about 0.7 to 0.8 per cent Once the desired acidity (0.7) is developed, the product should be shifted to cold store, (0°C).

Shrikhand

Shrikhand is semi-solid, sweetish-sour fermented milk product.

A fully mechanized/continuous process has been developed for industrial production of shrikhand by Aneja and Vyas (1983). Method employer by number of daries in Maharashtra and Gujrat (Sugum).

Technology

1. Preparation of curd: Skim milkj used which then pasteurized and allowed from for incubation by adding culture.

2. Preparation of chakka: Prepared by separating the whey from Delhi. Earlier 28" diameter basket centrifuge at 1100 RPM was used that produce 80 kg curd/hr. Now the process has been upgraded by using the quarg separator. It's capacity is 2500 kg of curd/hr.
3. Preparation of shrikhand from chakka: Add sugar then heatin SSHE after that add cream(80 per cent fat) so that 8.5 per cent fat in final product on DM basis.
4. The final product contains: 5 per cent fat, 42 per cent sugar and 60 per cent TS and protein 10.5 per cent. The acidity is in between 1.10 and 1.40 per cent.

The process of shrikhand manufacture has been upgraded further. In the modified process use of quark separator that can handle 25,00 kg of curd input/hr which permit the scale up production of 8 tonnes/hr.

Fat Rich Product-Ghee

- ☆ Ghee is clarified butter fat.
- ☆ Produced by heat desiccation of makkhan butter or cream.

Size of Industry

Production: 1.3 million tonnes

Value: 130 billion

Growth rate: 5 per cent

Organized prod.: 10 per cent

Mechanized Manufacture

First attempt at mechanized/continuous ghee manufacture was made in 1974 by Dr. Punjrath. Illustrates this method in which butter is taken as base material.

Industrial Process for Continous Production of Ghee, with Cream as Starting Material (Dr. Panjrath)

In this concentration of fat and breaking of fat-in-water emulsion is done mechanically with the help of centrifugal force in the clarifixator and concentrator, and the use of heat is limited to development of flavour and removal of traces of moisture. The plant requires low energy input and can be adapted for much larger

Convenience Dairy Products Development

New Product	*Used in*	*Technology*	*References*	*Remarks*
Channa powder	For sandesh	Try, roller, spray durying process	Tiwari *et al.* (1976)	Shelf life-2 to 4 month (air tight)
Dried channa like products	Dried rasgolla	Spry drying of UF skim milk mix with calculated fat	Dharam Pal *et al.* (1993)	Balanced flavour and spongy texture
Chakka powder		Dahi-removal of whey-Ground-Slurry-homogenization-spray driver.	De and Patel (1989)	TS-96.18, Fat-36.48 Protein-44.98, Red Sugar-11.53, Sucrose-Acidity-6.53
Lassi powder	In a beverage	Cure-agitaion-slurry-spray dried-dry blending sugar	Ladkani *et al.* (1993)	Moisture-5% Fat-29-31 Protein-23-24
Khoa powder	Khoa based sweet	Emulsifier Khoa-slurry—Mix Stabilizer (18% T5)-drum dired	Patel and De (1977)	Expensive energy intensive
Khoa powder	Khoa based sweet	Modified-milk conc (TS-28%)-Pan drying-Pulverization	Thompkinson dne De (1987)	Carry powdery taste
Khoa powder	Khoa based sweet	Used RO milk and then heat in thermulator	Razvi *et al.* (1987)	Burned flavour and caramal colour
Khoa powder	Khoa based sweet	Tray drying (70ºC for 4hr.) Roller drying Spray drying (190ºC and 78ºC)	Rangnodham (1988)	
Dry Gulab jamun mix	Gulabjamun (100 gm mix + 55 ml water)	SMP (43.4%) Maida (25%) Suji (15%) Butter fat (15%) Baking powder (1.5%) Cardamon (0.1%)	Ghpsh *et al.* (1986)	Shelf life 6 month

volumes. The process also results in lower SNF losses and better fat recovery.

Convenience Dairy Product Development

Due to production of convenience TDP it is possible

- ☆ To meet the seasonal and regional requirement
- ☆ Transport to big cities.
- ☆ Continuous packaging
- ☆ Uniform physico-chemical property and long shelf life.
- ☆ Will open new avenues for interstate marketing and trading overseas.
- ☆ Allows the housewife to make dairy product at home.

Conclusion

It is distinctly evedent from the foregoin discussion that the Indian dairy industry will have to rely more on traditional dairy products for its sustenance and development. At far as status of these products is concerned a good beginning has already been made but we have miles to go. Small scale manufacturers *i.e.* halwais are unaware about emerging trends in processing, quality control, packaging and fuel economy. The Indian dairy industry has been reluctant to switch from western dairy products over to the traditional dairy products mainly because the complete mechanized processes of manufacture of these products, except khoa, and packaging systems are not available. The unique flavour and texture of each TDP is probably another prominent stabling block in the mechanization of these products. The following strateries may be adopted to capitalize of the golden opportunity afforded by the GATT, and also keeping in view the changed situation of Indian dairy industry, globalization and entry of private sector and more demond for value added product.

- ☆ Large-scale production of TDP
- ☆ Maintaining high quality at every stage of milk touch
- ☆ Packaging of TDP should be strengthen
- ☆ Tremendous opportunity in the area of TDP should be seized
- ☆ The taste and food habit of overseas consumers should be investigated and included in our product mixes.

Chapter 4

Recent Innovation in Packaging of Milk and Milk Products

B.R. Ulmek
Head
Department of Animal Science and Dairy Science
M.P.K.V. Rahuri, Ahemadnager, M.S.

Package is the gateway to know a product. A product is often identified by the package in which it is served Packaging forms an integral part of food production, marketing and distribution. Packaging is the essential in a modern society, because one cannot store food, distribute it and keep it safe without packaging. The industry contributed 2 per cent. of the GDP and expects a higher demand for packing materials with an estimated requirement of 20 million tones by 2001 (Anonymous, 1998). In India improperly packaged foods undergo many flavour and textural changes during transportation and marketing. It is in this context that emphasis should be laid upon proper packaging methods for traditional milk products in India. Also in recent years the popularity for traditional products like ghee, paneer, rasogolla, burfi etc. have increased in European countries and lot of export potentials exit for these products.

India can now boast of an impressive array of dairy products manufactured within the country. With liberalization, the Indian industry seems to have suddenly moved into a state of high excitement. To have a greater share of the market every firm has started talking of new products and that means new packaging.Changes in demographic pattern, consumers habits, increased income, enhanced competition, introduction of new technologies and new expectation of the consumers, etc. are likely to give a new stimuli to packaging.

Any planning for interstate or export marketing of indigenous dairy products must take into consideration prioritization of packaging methods so that the quality and image of foods are improved. The changing lifesty, urbanization and increased consumerism have flooded the market with value-added, branded, and attractively packaged food products. Today, an arrary of packaging material and systems such as aseptic and retort packaging,gas/vaccum packing bag-in-box and lined carton systems, shrink wrapping of high barrier materials.Development of high barrier materials Controlled Atmosphere Packaging (CAP) or Modified Atmosphere Packaging (MAP) systems, aseptic packaging system and the like has changed the food marketing system, providing more "fresh food" in retail stores for a longer duration.

The four most important aspect of packaging are:

1. Presentation (graphics and material)
2. Cost
3. Consumer friendliness (Easy to open and use)
4. And effect on environment (Such packaging materials that can be recyled or reused)

The primary function of packaging material is to protect the product from diverse environmental conditions, *e.g.* O_2, light, moisture etc. and to supply information to the user about that products. The packaging present the product in an appealing manner and also influences the consumer's attitude in selecting that particular product rather than another, and the ultimate life of the product.

Packaging has become a social-scientific discipline with the modern role of:

1. Containing and safety that is supreme importance.
2. Facilitating the handling, storage and distribution.
3. Protecting against biological, chemical and distribution damages.

4. Providing convenience.
5. Informing through the medium of labeling.
6. Security through a tamper evident design.
7. Contributing to the product image through structural and graphic design.
8. Increasing the shelf life and ensuring longer availability.
9. As a marketing and advertising tool.
10. Environmental protection by taking responsibility of empty packaging after its use. (Patil, 2003)

Present Status of Food Packaging Industry in India

The packaging industry in India is a heterogeneous mix of both organized and unorganized sectors. It is estimated that during the year 1995 the money spent on packaging materials and packages alone amount to nearly Rs.29,000 million. Another 10,000 million is spent on packaging operations and related activities. And it is estimated that the amount can be doubled by the year 2000. The packaging materials manufactured by the industry are tinplate, aluminum, glass, plastic, paper and board, jute etc. (Dordi 1998)

The production of tinplate contains is estimated to be 0.46 million tones and more than 0.3 million tones are imported. Aluminum can used for carbonated drinks and beer accounts to 0.035 million tones. Aluminum foil accounts for 7000 tones. The production of glass bottles and hollow wares for packaging purpose is estimated to be 0.9 million tones. Paper and paperboards are also used in food industry as cartons in laminates as combibloe, aseptic cartons etc. corrugated fireboard boxes are the most popularly used media for distribution of goods are produced 0.9 million tones. (Patil,2003). It is estimated that by the year 2000 to pack 174 lakh tones of milk will packed. This will require 82,000 metric tones of polyethylene (Mathur,1998).

Selection/Choice of an Appropriate Packaging Material

The packages mainly perform three functions *viz.* to contain, to protect and to sell the product. An appropriate packaging material is governed by several factors such as - (Dhar,2000 and Aneja *et al.*, 2003).

1. It must provide barrier to light, temperature, gasses (oxygen, nitrogen and carbon dioxide) and moisture.
2. Weight and shape of the container.
3. Effect on filling and sealing speeds.
4. Contamination of food by constituents of the packing material.
5. Storage condition - How long the product needs to be protected.
6. Biodegradability and recycling potential.
7. Withstand to the transportation over long distances has become a necessity.
8. Milk being a highly perishable product utmost care is needed in its preservation during storage, handling and transportation.
9. The packaging material must be printable. Low in cost (Dhar, 2002 and Aneja *et al.*, 2003).

Range of Packaging Materials

The Packaging industry in India is still in the evolutionary stage. Altholugh the packaging industry is diverse, it uses only for basic materials namely glass, paper/board, metals and plastics. The common packaging material along with are listed below:

Basic Packaging Material Used for Food Packing

Packaging Material	*Use/Forms*
Paper	Bags, boxes, cartons, sacks, Cups
Glass	Bottles, jars tumblers,
Metal (Tin plated)	Can, aluminum foil, tray, lacquered can
Plastics	Pouches, cups, boxes, bottles
Laminates	Multilayered, cartons
Timber	Box, tub, cask or barrel
Clothes	Sack Special package
Wax	For coating
Edible	Special use for ice – cream cone.

Source: De, 1998; Aneja *et al.*, 2003.

Properties of Packaging Material

Sl.No.	Material	Advantages	Disadvantages
1	Paper (carton boards) Types; Craft paper, Brown paper, coated paper, Parchment, wax coated)	Cheapest among all Good environmental image Excellent Printability Biodegradable and renewable Ease of manufacture and light in weight Can used as Primary and Secondary container	Can be easily unsealed Poor moisture barrier Property Low tearing strength Poor in protective against gases,odours water and grease
2	Glass (Bottles, Tars)	Excellent visibility Strong, rigid and chemically inert Does not deteriorate Low WVTR Good Sealability Recyclable	Heavy Handing problem Frigidity Non biodegradable High transportation cost
3	Metal (Aluminum, can, steel)	Easy to airtight Good barrier against light, gasses and environmental effect Can be use in laminated films Good printability Good strength	High cost

Contd...

Table–Contd...

Sl.No.	*Material*	*Advantages*	*Disadvantages*
4	Plastics	Low weight as compared to PVC, PET	Gas permeability higher than PVC or PET
	A/PP	High tempe. Resistance	
		Low moisture permeability	
		Excellent stress crack property	
	B/PVC	Recyclable	Unsuitable for not filling
		Good rigidity	Problem of ecological disposal
		Good impact strength	High or permeability
	C/LDPE	Low permeability to water vapour and oxygen	Less barrier to light
		Good impact strength at low tempe.	
		Low moisture permeability	Had less stiffness than HDPE
		Co- extruded multiplayer films – widely used	
	D/HDPE	Excellent impact strength against mechanical stress and low tempe.	High Permeability of gases
		Low water vapour permeability	
		Lighter in weight	

De (1998) Nan do (2001). Montoya (2001) Panvalker and Caldwell (2002); Aneja *et al.* (2003).

Storage Taupe and Shelf Life of Traditional Milk Products in Different Packaging

Packaging Material	Temp. ºC	Storage Period (Days)	Reference
Fermented Milk Products			
Dahi			
Polystyrene (PS) Cup	+5*c	7	-
Polypropylene (PP) Cup	7	15	Mathur (1991)
Shrilhand			
Polystyrene (PP)	-10 to 18	6 months	Mathur (1991)
Lassi			
Pouch (LDPE)	+5	7	Cited Aneja *et al.* (2003)
Condensed Milk Products			
Khoa			
Tin	37	14	
Paper/Al. foil/LDPE or MST Cellulose/LDPE	37	10	Goyal and Rajorhia, 1991
PP/LDPE Al foil/LDPE	30	14	
PS/E VOH/PL	Cold storage	Longer period	Pal 2003
Pedha			
EVA/EVA/PVDC/EVA	20	30	Kumar *et al.* (1997)
MAP Packaging	37	2 months	
(Without Scavenger)			
MAP (with scavenger).	20	6months	Narwade , 2003
Vegetable Parchment	37+1	15 days	
Paper lined with card-board			
Burfi			
Pohster tub Vacuum	30	52	Patil and
Packaged in multilyer	-	16	Pal, 2000
Co-extryded nylon			
Pouch Without vacuum			
Packaged			

Contd...

Table 1.3–Contd...

Packaging Material	Temp. ºC	Storage Period (Days)	Reference
Gulabjamun			
Pohstyre ne (PP) cup	+5	30	Cited by Antenatal
Tins	Room Temp	270	(2003)
Coagulated Milk Products			
Paneer			
Cryovac Polyethylene (under vacuum packaging)	6+1	30	Sachdeva (1991)
EVA/EVA/PVDC/EVA	Refrigerated	90	Punjarath (1997)
PVC cling film	7+1	13	Kankhare (2004)
Chhama			
MST cellulose/LDPE	37	3	Pal (2003)
	Refrigerated	20	
Rasogolla			
Tins (Lacquered)	Room Temp	180	Cited by Aneja *et al.* (2003)
Fat- rich Milk Product			
Ghee			
Tin (Lacquered)	RoonTemp +5	180 270	Cited by Aneja *et al.* (2003)
Pouched (Bag inbox)	Room Temp	180	

Recent Packing Techniques

Aseptic Packing

Aseptic packaging is a relatively new packaging concept may defined as a packaging process in which a presterilized and sterile produced is filled under sterile conditions into sterile packages in a sterile environment and then germproof sealed.

The major requirement of an aseptic packaging unit is to prevent recontamination of the sterilized product. The principal considerations in this regard include sterilization of filling machine and packaging material by suitable physical or chemical means and maintaining aseptic barriers during filling and sealing (Singh, 2003).

Modified Atmosphere Packaging

MAP is a process by which the shelf life of the fresh product is increased significantly by enclosing it an atmosphere, which slows down the spoilage process.

MAP is the most advanced food preserving technique with many advantages. This method of packaging replaces the air headspace of package with a specific food grade gas or mixture of gases. It retards the growth of mould and bacteria besides reducing the oxidative deterioration and preventing mechanical damage to the product by adding cushion of gas around the product

MAP slows respiration rates, reduces microbial growth and retards enzyme spoilage with the final effect of lengthening the shelf life of the product. Generally, three types of gas mixtures (N_2, CO_2 and O_2) are used in Map at modifying level.

Packaging Material

The packaging material must have low water vapour transmission rate with high gas barrier capacity. It must have mechanical strength to withstand machine handling and subsequent storage, distribution and retailing. Strength, impermeability and heat sealability character are found in laminated film. The packaging of non-respiring product include nylon/PE/nylon/PVDC/PE or nylon/EVOH/PE.Strength is provided by outmost layer of nylon and moisture vapour impermeability is provide by EVOH or PVDC and heat salability is provided by PE. (Kanawjia, 2003).

Vacuum Packaging

This process is useful to extend the shelf life of perishable products without addition of preservatives. The purpose of this packaging is to delay microbiological, no microbiological deterioration of the product and thereby increase its shelf life. It removes air from the package with no gas replacement resulting in skin-tight film package. In normal packaging, the presence of oxygen in the air causes oxidation of fat. By elimination air, in effect oxygen, through Vacuum packaging, the product spoilage is checked and its shelf life is increased. When paneer is packed in high barrier film (EVA/PVDC/EVA) under Vacuum and heat sealed at 90°C for one minute, its shelf life is extended to 90 days at the refrigeration temperature. Vacuum packaging has recently been used to extend the shelf life of fried paneer. Though it is also useful in extending the shelf life of Peda, it made pedas stick together and loose their shape and hence found unsuitable (Aneja *et al.*, 2003)

Oxygen Absorbers/Scavengers

Oxygen absorbers are composed of substances chemically reactive to oxygen. These include reduced iron, reactive dyes, ascorbic acid, and glucose oxidase and alcohol oxidase immobilized on the inner surface of the films. These are packaged in gas permeable materials in the form of small packets. When placed in a closed container (thin, pouch), the oxygen absorber packet completely removes oxygen from the air within the container and thus extends the shelf life of the product. These absorbers also called scavengers, have a great potential for extending the shelf life of whole milk powder/infant foods, cheese, peda, ghee and many Indian sweets.

Oxygen absorbers, without mixing with the packaged foods, protect them from oxygen damages such as taste and flavour deterioration, oxidation discoloration and growth of moulds and insects. These scavengers also guard against the possible loss of any vitamins, such as C,E, and A that are sensitive to oxidation.

This technology has been successfully utilized for extending the shelf life of peda at the Sumul Dairy, Surat. Peda when packed in barrier film with oxygen scavenger and indicator tablet to rated the concentration level of oxygen in the pack and stored at 37°C, ambient temperature, and at 20°C, showed the shelf life of two months, five months and six months respectively. However, the product could become brown because of the Maillard reaction when stored for long time at a higher temperature. (Aneja *et al.*, 2003 and Singh, 2003).

Edible Packaging

The edible film development is still in nascent stage. The edible film or coating is a thin layer of edible material formed on, placed on or between the foods or food components. The package is an integral part of the food product. The greatest advantage is that most of edible films are biodegradable, leading to reduce solid waste and environmental pollution. When protein edible coatings are now being developed to extend the shelf life of oxygen sensitive foods like nuts, reduce moisture loss, respiration and ripening rate in fresh fruits and vegetables and reduce packaging costs (Banerjee, 1995, Kanawjia, 2003).

Poly-clip System

The poly clip system is the basis of new packaging concept. The material is filled into a tube which is formed from the reel stock via a forming shoulder and sealed along the side. Simultaneously, it is filled automatically and closed by two aluminum clips in rhythm of the desired production cycle. This type of packaging can be used for emulsions like butter, cheese, cheese foods, cheese ice cream, mozzarella cheese and can replace metal, glass coated card boare, plastic containers and minimize the amount of packaging as well as reduce the strain on environment which is a hot nowadays.

Self-heating Packages

The packages, invariably, are of double construction. The inner tray of the lower portion includes separate sections of exothermic agents (calcium, aluminum, mangling and water).

When the separation between the 2 sections is broken by an exothermic reaction heats up the food in the upper chamber.

Bio-degradable Polymer Packaging Materials

These are some successful attempts for their development like the 'BIOPOL' (ployhydroxy butyrate) and bio-degradable polymer containing 6 per cent corn starch. A photo-degradable plastics that degrades within 120 days when exposed to sunlight and useful for food packaging is also reported.

Use of Artificial Intelligence

Software package are now available which automate the process of designing a food package. Packaging Advisor TM a system software is developed by Du pont to evaluate and help select appropriate package design structural and barrier resin materials for a given application under given constraints like specified limits on total oxygen permeation, humidity (inside and outside the package), water vapour transmissions properties, of each layer within the package, compatibility with intended fabrication process, optical clarity, regulatory agency status, sterilization and a number of similar parameter.

The software package determines the required thickness of the barrier layer, and the material costs and ranks the alternate designs with the least cost the first (Punjrath, 1995).

Conclusion

Technological progress and revolutionary improvements are taking place at a very fast speed in the packaging. New systems, materials, machinery, designs, printing and labeling and environmental concerns are some innovations in the dairy packaging sector. These innovations have provided greater convenience to consumers, extended the shelf life of products, lowered costs and also led improvements in sales, better hygienic conditions and handling.

LDPE/LDPE + BUTENE is best suited for packaging of milk. Multilayer films are also used for the packaging of milk products(PR, RP, PS, with paper board or aluminum) in the form of cartons. High pressure steam is used to sterilize product lines and H_2O_2 with heat of UV radiation for container materials. Ethylene vinyl alcohol (EVOH) has excellent gas barrier properties in dry condition and suitable for packaging of milk sweets such as Peda and burfi under vacuum or MAP. Many innovations have taken place in packaging systems in the past, such as. Modified atmospheric packaging (MAP), vacuum packaging, aseptic packaging and oxygen scavengers. These synergistic effects, along with appropriately chosen packaging material, on the shelf life and could have great prospects in the packaging of traditional Indian dairy products.

References

Anonymous, 1998.Industry News. Processed Food Industry.19(2):45

Aneja, R. P., Mathur, B. N., Chandan, R. C. and Banerjee, A. K.2003. Technology of Indian Milk Products 1st Edn. A Dairy India Publication. 293-307.

Arora,S, Naylae, S.K. and Sindhu, J.S.2000. Dairy packaging for the fruture. Beverage and Food World. 27 (9) 41-42.

Banerjee, r. 1995. Edible films and coatings. Indian Dairyman. 41(7),22-25.

Bhattacharya, G.K.2000. CAP and MAP. Processed Food Industry. 3(1) : 23-24.

Biradar, U.S., Dev, D.K., and Ingale, U.M. 1985. Shelf-life extension of Pedha by Packaging. J.Food Sci.50. 51-54.

Dhar, R.2002. New packaging materials and packaging technology for dairy products. Indian Dairyman.54(2) 72-75.

Dordi,M.C.,1998.Packing of edible oils, vanaspati and ghee-an overview in modern food packaging.Publ.Indian Institute of packaging, Mumbai,pp.492-505

Goyal, G.K. and Raorhia, G.S. 1991. Role of modern packaging and marketing of indigenous dairy products. Indian Food Industry. July-Aug.32-34.

Kanawji, S.K.2003. Modified atmosphere packaging for dairy and food aindustry. A compendium of Advances in dairy and food products, Fev.13th –March 5th, NDRI, Karnal

Kankhare, D.H. 2004. Studies on preservation of paneer. Ph.D.Thesis. Unpublished. M.P.K.V., Rahuri, Ahemadnager (MS).

Kaushik, S. 1998. Recent innovation in the packaging of liquid milk-Fino. Indian Dairyman. 50(12) 128-131.

Kumar, R. Bandyopadhyay, Punjarth, J.S.1997. Shelf-life extension of pedha using different packaging techniques. Indian J.Dairy Sci. 50(1) 40-49.

Mathur, Meena. 1998. Packaging of fresh milk in flexible pouches. IndianDairyman.50(12)199-121

Moitreyee. 2001. packaging materials for food industry properties and desigen. Beverages and Food World. 28(8) 27.

Nando, G.B. 2001. Polymer blends in Packaging industry. The present statues and future prospectus. Indian Food Industry. 28(8)39-42.

Nandu, P.K. and Snyal, M. K.2001. Packaging material and potential source for tainting of food products. Processed Food Industry. 5(2) 10-14.

Narayanan, C.K.2001. Trends in health food drinks packaging. Indian Food Industry. 20(2) 60-62.

Narwade S. G., 2003. Effect of processing and copositional variable on the quality oy pedha. Ph.D. Thesis submitted to MPKV,Rahuri Ahmednager.

Pal, D.2003. Packaging of traditional Indian Dairy Products. Present status and future prospectus. A Compendium of Advances in dairy food products, Feb. 13th – March 5th, NDRI, Karnal.

Panvalkar, S.G. Askalti Caldwell. 2002. Making your packging environmentaly friendly. Beverage and Food World 29(1)60.

Sachdeva,S;Propek,D and Reuter,H.1991.Technology of paneer from cow milk.Jap.J.Dairy foodsci.,40(2):a855555-a97

PunJarath,S.J.1995.Trends in packaging of milk and milk products.India Dairyman.47(50);29-40

Patil,G. R.2003Statis of packaging in India A Compodium of Advances in dairy and food products, Feb13-March 5 NDRI,Karnal.

Chapter 5

Man Power for Indian Milk Products: Present Availability and Future Demand

V.N. Bhargava

Retired Professor, A.H. and Dairying, BHU, Varanasi
Director, K.S. Singhal Dairies Pvt Ltd., Agra

Introduction

Though it is difficult to rely on statistics because there is a famous statement, "torture the data long enough and it will confess to anything", it is an exception in the present case as these are untutored and from an independent and reliable publication (Dairy India publications).

Traditional Indian Dairy products had and still have significance in our life:

Social Life

No feast, festival or wedding take place without milk based sweets. Packs of "sandesh" are used to convey or disclose good news.

Religious Ceremony

Milk products (dahi; khoa, ghee) are used as offerings in religious ceremonies.

Health and Nutrition

Provide health promoting nutrients and some of these (fermented products with probiotics) have additional therapeutic values and immunity stimulating effects.

Economic Life

50 to 55 per cent (approximately 42 million ones) of milk produced in the country is converted into Indian milk products, which is estimated at Rs.400 billion. Share of the organized sector in the indigenous products is at present only Rs.50 billion, but is expected to rise rapidly in the coming years.

Table 5.1: Projected Demand for Major Milk Products in the Organized Sector (Anon, 2003)

Product	*Demand 1998 (Metric Tonnes)*	*Project Demand 2009 (Metric Tonnes)*
Ghee	100,000	200,000
Shrikhand	3,000	5,650
Rasogolla	1,600	6,000
Gulabjamun	3,000	5,850

Scenario Shift Augmenting Demand

Combined effects of the following are moulding the market profile of the indigenous milk products:

1. Increased urbanization and income growth are taking rapid strides in the country. It is projected that the percentage of urban population will increase from the present 27.8 (in 2001) to 33.8 in 2016. Our Tenth Five Year Plan (2002-2007) has been formulated on the Prime Minister's vision of doubling the per capita income within the next10 years by keeping the GDP growth at 8 per cent during 2002-2007 and 9.3 per cent during the 11th Five Year Plan period. It is envisaged that the percentage of population in the lower income group (below Rs.22,500 per annum) will decrease from 53.6 (in 1994-95) to 17.8 in 2006-07 year and percentage in middle (Rs.45,000 – 70,000) income group will grow from 11.2 to 20.5 and in the high income (above Rs.96,000) from 2.9 to 11.7 during the same

period (NCAER survey and estimate, National Milk Seminar, 1999-2000). It is well known that the rich class in India consumes milk largely as liquid or in the form of products while in the lower income groups use it as whitener in tea or coffee. As the income rises, the consumer expenditure on milk and products increases, the consumption preference shifts from liquid milk to curd, makkhan, ghee, mithais, paneer and so on. With urbanization and consequent increase in disposable income, the demand for value added foods, largely in favour of dairy products is fast spinning off.

2. Changing life styles with growing proportion of working women becoming part of urban population having extended working hours due to long distance travel to reach work place, are leading to an increased demand for convenient ready to use innovative food products. This in turn, has resulted in increasing demand for packaged dairy products (traditionally prepared at home) *e.g.* Paneer curry, kadhi mix, kheer mix, dahi, shrikhand.

3. A market for Indian Milk based sweets is developing oversees. There is continuous rise in ethnic population throughout the world and India is among the top four nations sending largely skilled immigrants abroad. This in turn is creating considerable growth in demand for ethnic food everywhere. In North America alone, the market for Indian milk sweets is estimated at $500 million. Twenty million Indian over half of them living in the west, are part of the upper income group. The Indian Diaspora presents an exciting avenue for globalization of mithais. Entrepreneurs in Europe, North America and Australia are looking into the prospects of manufacturing them. Good commercial market for Indian milk sweets is emerging in the developed countries where the share of food in the total household expenditure is small (anon, 2003). A recent consumer Research report compiled for a US food chain has projected that the Indian foods is likely to rule the roost (Banerjee, 2002). This is just to give an idea about the impending markets of ethnic food vis-à-vis Indian sweets emerging in USA alone, leaving aside the markets in other countries.

4. The growing health awareness amongst consumers is surfacing demands for nutritive foods. On this basis dairy projects enjoy a positive image in terms of quality and health benefits. Fermented milk products like dahi, yogurts, buttermilk are considered health promoting. Dissemination of information that manufacture of traditional milk products does not involve the use of chemical or any preservative is giving added boost to this demand.
5. Realization amongst the business class that the traditional milk products not only enjoy mass appeal but also have higher operating margins than the western dairy products, mainly due to lower raw material cost is having a favourable impact on the expanding market. It is estimated that the raw material costs of Shrikhand, Rasogolla, Gulabjamun, khoa sweets, Sandesh and Paneer are 29 per cent, 33 per cent, 34 per cent, 35 per cent and 65 per cent of the sale price respectively. For western dairy products, comparative costs are relatively higher varying from 7-80 per cent (Patil, 2002).

Thus, in store is a bright future for these products which present a great opportunity for the organized dairies to modernize and scale up the production of these.

Popular Traditional Dairy Products

A variety of intermediate traditional dairy products are produced in India. Some of which are used as base for making sweets by the halwais in cities. On the basis of unit operations used, these can be classified as:

1. *Heat desiccation*: Khoa, Khurchan, Rabri
2. *Acid Coagulation*: Channa, Paneer
3. *Lactic Acid Fermentation*: Dahi, Lassi, Misti Doi, Chakka
4. *Fat Churning*: Makkhan
5. *Heat Clarification*: Ghee
6. *Freezing*: Kulfi
7. *Cooking (Milk based desserts)*: Kheer, Phirni, payassam, sevian.

Man Power Requirement for Milk Product Manufacture

Operations which require manual labour in organized indigenous products manufacture are collection, reception, weighment, testing, chilling, standardization and pasteurization of milk and for other specific operations according to the product to be prepared. Manpower is also required for operating boiler, refrigeration plant and stand-by diesel generators and for accounts, purchase, sales and administrative jobs.

Requirement of manpower will vary according to the extent and efficiency of mechanization available at the plant. Traditional methods with no mechanization require more manual labour. No documented data on the personnel required for indigenous milk products manufacture are available. However, Aneja *et al.* (2002, p 229) have estimated that the personnel requirements of the dairy which will handle 20,000 kg of milk per day at 39, which includes:

- ☆ One General Manager
- ☆ Two managers (production and administrative)
- ☆ Four Assistant Managers (Marketing, Quality Control, Accounts, Purchase)
- ☆ Six Office Administration (1 steno, 4 office assistants, 1 peon); and
- ☆ Twenty workers

In other words, 13 technically qualified and 26 other workers are needed.

Considering that the organized sector is handling 5.2 million ones of milk per annum for making the Indian milk products, at this rate the present requirement of technically qualified persons in dairy technology works out to 9,260 and that of other workers comes to 18,520. In the coming 5 years, the organized sector will manufacture twice the present production; technically qualified people needed will be approximately 10,000 or say 2000 per year.

At present there are 13 Dairy Science colleges and several state owned polytechnic institutes producing nearly 300 degree and diploma holders per year in dairy technology (Khan, 2004; Bandopadhayay, 2004). Obviously, the country will be facing a shortage of dairy manufacturing professionals as the targeted expansion in dairy sector at 8 per cent per year takes place.

References

Anon (2003) Tradition reinvented; Times Food Processing Journal 3(1) p20-24

Aneja, R.P., Mathur, B.N., Chandan, R.C., Banerjee, A.K. (2002) Technology of Indian Milk Products, Pub. Dairy India

Bandopadhyay, A.K. (2004) Vision of dairy technology Education and Research; Indian Dairyman 56(10) p 98-101

Banerjee, A (2002) President's Desk, Indian Dairyman 54(10) p3-4

Khan, A.Q. (2004) Dairy Education in India: Vision 2020; Indian Dairyman 56(10) p96-97

Patil, G.R. (2002) Present status of traditional dairy products; Indian Dairyman 54(10) 35-46.

Chapter 6

Tailoring Training Curriculam Based on Indian Milk Products Industrial Needs

V.N. Bhargava

Retired Professor, A.H. and Dairying, BHU, Varanasi

Director, K.S. Singhal Dairies Pvt Ltd., Agra

Introduction

At the outset, this is not a lecture, not even a talk; it is only a mechanism of sharing thoughts with you, based on my experiences as a "hands-on" executive in the Indian dairy industry.

For any industry to flourish and remain competitive, besides a strategic evolving technology, efficient machine and man power constitute the most important inputs. With rapid urbanization and rise in disposable income for the masses in the country, rapid growth in demand for traditional milk products is taking place. Export of Indian milk products and sweets had been started with a modest earning of Rs.326 million in the year 1995-96 (Rajorhia, 2001). With the liberalization of agricultural trade under the new GATT regime, the heavy subsidies prevalent in the dairy sector in the countries of EU and USA will be brought down in the next few years. This competitive advantage of the Indian dairy industry will then have new vistas for export of dairy commodities (Saravana Kumar and Jain, 2004).

According to the Tenth Five Year Plan (2002-2007) document (p568) also there is a tremendous potential for the Indian dairy products in the export market in Asian and African countries. Undoubtedly, therefore, large scale commercialization of traditional milk products has bright prospects and future. Nevertheless, threats posed by liberalization cannot be ignored. Some of the developed countries, as part of their product diversification have been doing a lot of research and development activities on ethnic foods, which include Indian dairy products. For instance, Ghee is one of our age old milk products, but Australia has now become an important exporter of it (Banerjee, 2002). For survival and to remain competitive, continuous upgrading of man, machine, process and technology has become imperative for our dairy sector to cash on these opportunities and face the challenges. Business man's concept of what has been earned per rupee invested has to be given a back seat. And considering the socio economic development and life style becoming fast and time demanding, the performance should be rated in terms of profit earned per man-hour spent in work. Implementation of this, demands staffing the organization properly with qualified trained and experienced personnel at all levels.

Proper Training – Today's Need for Human Resource Development

Human resource development is a continuous and sustained exercise to prepare individuals with proper training and motivation to eliminate future crisis. Educational designing and redesigning aimed at coping with the task in foreseeable future in order to provide opportunities according to aptitude and ability and for service to the society is a dynamic process. Human resource is an unseen but ultimate resource of a nation. Investment in human development is, therefore, considered more productive than investment in physical assets so the former leads to faster rate of national progress, if the same is done in a systematic way and without degeneration (Nagarcenkar, 1990).

Present Scenario and Future Demand Trend

There is a marked spurt in the growth of organized dairy sector. Already there is also a global interest in this sector mainly due to the fast expanding urban consumer market in India which is likely to grow to size of 350-400 million during the next five years (Mathur,

2000). A number of multinational companies are coming up in the organized sector with aggressive plans for marketing dairy products. Consequent to the current social economic outlook, significant modifications in the consumer's taste and preferences is coming forth and creating ample scope for developing newer range of dairy products. In the immediate future, greater emphasis would be placed on products that provide health and nutritional benefits in addition to satisfaction of the taste buds. Dairy research would assume greater strategic significance. This needs to be oriented in such a manner so as to impart further opportunities for value addition and novelty in respect of consumer convenience, quality assurance, nutritional information conforming to the international standards and trends. This presents new challenges of complying with good manufacturing practices, competitiveness in processing, economies and strategic marketing. Further, emergence of new technological processes such as fractionations, electro-dialysis and membrane filtrations have made milk an important industrial liquid whose valuable ingredients can be extracted and recombined in various ways to form new products. Using these technologies, dairy plants in future will be manufacturing enriched products containing more calcium or other minerals, vitamins and elected fat fractions. Cholesterol-free, lactose–free and sugar-free milk products for diabetics will be available. Even health fitness stimulating products and anti-carcinogenic factor added milk products etc. will be made. All these will not be possible unless we have adequately trained manpower. Our HRD programme should be tailored to meet these challenges.

The present 13 Dairy Science Colleges along with state owned diploma awarding institutions though are producing approximately 250-300 degree and diploma holders every year in Dairy Technology they do not fulfill the requirement of the industry. Most of these remain either unemployed or under employed (Khan, 2004). The reason for such a situation is either these individuals do not come up to expectations of the industry or these are more than the number required. Both may be true.

In this context the fact should not be lost that over 85 per cent of the milk produced in the country is still handled by the unorganized dairies which mostly employ low wage workers, skilled labourers or technicians and not highly paid qualified professionals. Consequently demand for low paid skilled personnel is greater than for the educated degree holders. Similar is the assessment in the Tenth Five Year Plan (2002 – 2007) document which states that simultaneous with the incidence of rising unemployment among those with higher education, is also the shortage of trained technicians, accountants and other commercial assistants and skilled labourers. Dairy industry in India is presently having a growth rate of 4.7 percent per annum and is targeted to achieve 8 per cent per annum in this decade to boost up the share of milk products export from the present 1 per cent of the world market to about 20 per cent by 2020. Shift in greater proportion of milk handled by unorganized sector to the organized will take place and will directly reflect in creating increased job opportunities for the properly trained manpower.

Withdrawal of ICAR governance from Dairy Diploma awarding Institutes and expansion in quantity have been accompanied by fall in quality of training. In general, there is need of radical transformation in the dairy manufacturing education. Assertion of dignity of labour and vocationalization of curricula are essential to ensure that disjunction does not take place between the educational system and the work place. This needs immediate attention and corrective measures in modernization of syllabi, examination reforms, overcoming the problem of inadequate provision of budgetary resources from the government.

Educational programmes for dairy manufacturing should match future industrial needs. The education system should be capable of making the youth not only knowledgeable but also creative, motivated, dedicated, appreciative of dignity of labour and confident to take up self employment. Dairy products training organizations should empower the students to practice "earn while you learn and learn while you earn" and learning places should have sufficient linkages with the industrial organizations.

Proposal

Thus the dairy manufacturing industry has demands for the following and proper training curricula should be available for these?:

1. *Skilled Workers*: for manning the front floor level.
2. *Technicians*: for middle level floor shop jobs
3. *Professional*: for senior level day-to-day management

4. *Senior Professionals*: Professional specialists for specialized jobs of research planning, decision making and consultancy.

For Skilled Workers

Certificate course to impart knowledge in milk hygiene, plant sanitation, handling of milk factory equipment and machines. Short duration programme with more practical training.

For Technicians

Separate diploma course of 2½ years duration with 6 months in-plant workshop training in two streams:

1. *Dairy Engineering*: with courses and practical on basis of milk composition; milk products making; mechanical, electric and electronic jobs and sufficient information on refrigeration, steam, energy generating and using machines, packaging systems and operation and maintenance of packaging systems.
2. *Dairy Processing and Manufacturing*: Designed to offer information in basics of dairy engineering, dairy chemistry, microbiology, mathematics, dairy technology, milk product economics, accounting and business management and information technology.

For Professionals

Degree course of 3 ½ years duration with six months in-plant/ workshops training in two separate branches as for technicians mentioned above for imparting in-depth knowledge in courses. In addition courses on dairy business legal reform, export policies, organic dairy products. Yoga should be included.

For Senior Professionals

Post graduate degree course of 2 years duration, to enable specialization in one of the branches with greater emphasis on research and innovation.

Educational institutions should arrange linkages in these levels of dairy education to enable opportunity to individuals to better the qualifications and acquire knowledge of the technological innovations so that they can stay with the changes which industry would adopt. No progressive organization can afford to resist technology innovation. Individuals who do not continue their learning process to improve their skills will lose out in today's competitive market. The future of dairy industry depends upon the education and training of dairy professionals. The curriculum which the students will follow in professional career will significantly mould the future generations of dairy professionals. It is, therefore, highly essential to have a well structured committee representing Universities, Researchers and Dairy Industry executives to be involved to formulate details of curricula for dairy technology education and upgrade the same from time-to-time to meet the changing global perspective (Bandopadhyay, 2004).

References

Banerjee, A (2002) President's Desk, Indian Dairyman 54(10) p3-4

Bandopadhyay, A.K. (2004) Vision of dairy technology Education and Research; Indian Dairyman 56(10) p 98-101

Khan, A.Q. (2004) Dairy Education in India: Vision 2020; Indian Dairyman 56(10) p96-97

Mathur, B.N. (2002) Dairy Education and Research; Vision for the next millennium. Indian Dairyman 52(1) p 39-43

Nagarcenkar, R (1990) Dairy production education in a changing world from perspective of developing countries; Indian Dairyman 42(11) p 460-464

Rajorhia, G.S. (2001) Opportunities for dimensional growth of Indian Dairy processing industry; Indian Dairyman 53(9) pp 35-42.

Sarvanakumar, V. and Jain, D.K. (2004) Legal aspects of economic reforms in Indian dairy sector; Indian Dairyman 56(11) 56-64.

Chapter 7

Fermented–Milk Based Salted Indian Preparations

V.N. Bhargava

Retired Professor, A.H. and Dairying, BHU, Varanasi
Director, K.S. Singhal Dairies Pvt Ltd., Agra

Introduction

Fermented milks refer to those milks making of which involves the use of selected micro-organisms to develop the characteristic flavour, body and texture. The term fermentation relates to the metabolic process in which chemical changes are brought about on an organic substance whether protein, carbohydrate or fat through the action of enzymes produced by specific living micro-organisms. In milk product manufacturing, the most important fermentation is lactic acid fermentation, which is also referred to as "milk souring".

In India, fermented milk products such as dahi (curd), lassi (churned sweetened curd), chhach (buttermilk) occupy a prominent place in the people's diet. Besides imparting nutrition, these products assist greatly to preserve the fluid milk which otherwise would deteriorate rapidly under high ambient temperature. These are much more palatable than milk. Therapeutic significance of these products is considered more important than their nutritional value. Regular intake of these products increases concentration of lactic acid bacteria in the intestines, prevents gas forming putrefaction and arrests digestive disorders. It has been well established that individuals who suffer from lactose (milk-sugar) intolerance (or allergy) characterized by distressing symptoms of flatulence and and iarrhea on consuming milk can digest and tolerate these products well.

Lactic acid bacteria in the gut also have anti tumor and hypo-cholesterolic effects (Hosono, 2000). Besides, the fermentation taking place during their making brings about partial splitting of proteins, greater availability of calcium present in milk and production of water soluble vitamins leading to enhanced nutritional benefits. Regular consumption of some fermented milk products claimed to increase longevity of human being. In India, fermented milk products are used as such or as preparations both sweetened as well as salted types. Broadly, the fermented milk based products and preparations can be classified as follows:

Sweetened/Plain Unsweetened

Dahi (curd), Misti Dahi, Lassi, Srikhand, Srikhand wadi, probiotic kulfi.

Salted

Mattha/Chhach/Chhas; Raita, kadhi, dahi-vada, Curd-rice.

Mattha/Chhach/Chhas

Mattha, chhach or chhas are synonyms for buttermilk which is a byproduct obtained in the preparation of *makkan* from *dahi* by traditional process which involves churning a dahi and cold water mixture. It is preferred for its aroma and mildly sour proteolytic taste developed due to predominantly lactic acid fermentation. In Kerala, thin buttermilk produced by churning high acid curd is called "moru", which is consumed mixed with rice and pickle. When moru is diluted with water to lower its acidity and flovoured with salt, crushed ginger, curry leaves and green chillies, the product is called *Sambharam*, which is popular in southern states of the country (Aneja *et al.*, 2002 p. 179).

Method of Manufacture

Boiled or pasteurized milk is inoculated with dahi @ 1.0 – 1.5 per cent. Allowed to set overnight at 22-25°C. Fresh cold water is added to this dahi which is then stirred using "mathani" (wooden stirrer) till grains of makkhan are formed. These are scooped out and the resulting residual watery fluid is consumed as chhach or matha after addition of salt and ground roasted cumin. It contains 6-7 per cent milk solids and 1-2 percent fat.

Raita

Raita is prepared from dahi and is served along with wheat roti as part of meals.

Technology

Dahi is stirred and if necessary a small quantity of milk may be added to develop soft consistency. Salt, black pepper, fried mustard seeds or roasted ground cumin seeds are added along with besan (gram flour) granules. For making these granules, batter of besan is prepared by taking 100 gram of besan in 100 ml of water. The mixture is beaten to incorporate air and ¼ tea spoon of salt and ¼ teaspoon of baking powder are added. The batter is run through a perforated mould dye in a frying pan containing oil and granules are fried at 185°C till a light brown colour. Before mixing in dahi these are soaked in lukewarm water. This mixture is then garnished with red chilly powder and chopped mint and coriander leaves.

Variations

To the beaten dahi base, instead of besan granules following optional ingredients can be used for raita making:

1. Boiled diced potatoes
2. Raw Onion pieces and tomatoes
3. Raw grated cucumber and carrots
4. Boiled grated/mashed pumpkin or bottle guord
5. Boiled bathua leaves
6. Fresh mint leaves after grinding
7. Pieces of lady finger (okra) after light frying to make "pachadi" raita. (Aneja *et al.*, 2002 p182).

Kadhi

Kadhi is prepared from dahi or buttermilk in combination with besan throughout our country. Its composition varies from region to region. Milk solid content in Kadhi varies from 6-8 per cent and other solids remain in the range of 6-7 per cent.

For making Kadhi, dahi is prepared from milk standardized to 0.8–1.0 per cent fat. Milk is pasteurized/boiled and cooled to 37°C and inoculated with mixed culture of streptococcus thermophilus, lactococcus lactis and lactococcus cremories. Incubated till acidity of 0.95 per cent, fermented dahi is then stirred in a mixer. Bengal gram flour at 5 percent level of dahi along with an equal quantity of water is added. The mixture is then heated to boil. At this stage, appropriate quantity of turmeric powder, salt and spices are added and boiling continued for 10–15 minutes more till the total solids increase to 14–16 per cent.

Kadhi Powder or Dehydrated Kadhi

To make dried kadhi, the slurry without spices or fried besan balls obtained by the aforesaid process is cooled to 60°C and dried on a double drum drier (with roller speed at 16-20 rpm and steam pressure of 40-50 PSI). Addition of various spices like dried chillie powder, mustard or cumin seeds into slurry before drying should be avoided because it causes serious colour defects. These should be added when reconstituting the dehydrated kadhi. For reconstitution, one part of kadhi powder is to be mixed with 4 parts of boiled water. The ratio can vary according to viscosity preference. Cut vegetables and curry leaves may be added before boiling and fried beasan balls (pakoras) after boiling (Ghosh and Kulkarni, 1990; Aneja et al, 2002, p181). The kadhi powder when packed in L.D. Polyethylene pouches keeps well for up to 12 weeks.

Pouched Kadhi

Kadhi has also been made using cheese whey, chana dal powder, a mix of spices and a dash of ghee and is marketed in pouches by Amul.

Dahi Vada (Bhalla)

Dahi Vada is popular as a snack and is available at many fast food small vendors. It may be classed as a variation of raita. In its preparation, deep fried dal batter patties after soaking in water are dipped in dahi, instead of besan batter granules or vegetables.

There are two variations of dahi vada according to the material used to make the patties. The first one consists of soaking a mixture (1:1) of both gram (*Cicer arietimum*) and urad (*Phaseolus mungo*) dals in water overnight. Instead of mixture of these two pulses, only Moong

(*Phaseolus aureus* Roxb.) dal can be used. After removing the skin grinding of the dal/mix is done to get a thick paste. For every 500 grams of dal(s), ½ teaspoonful of garam masala, 500 gram dahi, requisite quantities of frying oil, ginger, salt and chilli powder are taken. Spices are mixed in the batter which is then whipped to incorporate air. The thickened batter is shaped into patties (5-6 cm diameter and 1-2 cm thick). These are then fried at 185°C until light golden brown and soaked in salted water for 15-20 minutes. After squeezing to remove excess water and oil, these patties are immersed in dahi which has been earlier whipped or beaten to a thinner consistency and spiced in a separate dish. Garnishing may be done with roasted cumin seed powder, red chilli powder, chopped coriander and mint leaves. Sweet sour tamarind sauce is poured over before serving.

In the second variation, Urad dal and ground coconut are used. Preparation consists of soaking 250 grams of urad dal, grinding and proceeding as described above up to frying of balls or patties. Base material consists of 1 kg of beaten dahi or buttermilk and 250 grams of finely grated coconut along with salt and seasonings. Fried mustard seeds and hot pepper chillies may be added to this. Fried balls or patties are then immersed in this for 2-3 hours after which these are ready to be served with desired garnishings, sauces and condiments.

Curd Rice

Curd rice is a popular south Indian diet containing cooked rice and dahi (curd) with added salt and spices to taste. The consistency of curd rice varies from flowable to semi solid mass. Common ingredients used are cooked rice, salt, and filling materials like chopped onions, mustard seeds, curry leaves, cut green chillies and ginger added as garnishings. Curd rice contains 2–3 per cent fat, 2.5–3.5 per cent proteins, 15–25 per cent total solids, 1–1.5 per cent ash and 9–14 per cent carbohydrates. The shelf life of curd rice packed in polyethylene pouches varies from 2–4 days at 6–8°C and 1–2 days at ambient temperature (Rashmi *et al.*, 2003).

References

Aneja, R.P., Mathur, B.N., Chandan, R.C., and Banerjee, A.K. (2002) Technology of Indian Milk Products, A Dairy India Publication, Delhi, India.

Ghosh, B.C. and Kulkarni, S. (1990) Dehydrated Kadhi: A convenience food. Indian Dairyman, 42(1): 11-14

Hosmo, A. (2002) Fermented Milk products and their impact on human health, particularly cancer, Indian Dairyman 54(11) 44-50

Rashmi, B.S., Ghosh, B.C., Kulkarni, S., Rao, K.J., and Balasubramanyam. (2003) Quality evaluation of curd rice sold in Bangalore market, Indian Journal of Dairy Sciences 56(5), 295-299.

Chapter 8

Emergence of Innovative Filled Indian Milk Products

V.N. Bhargava

Retired Professor, A.H. and Dairying, BHU, Varanasi
Director, K.S. Singhal Dairies Pvt Ltd., Agra

Introduction

Clarified milk fat or ghee usually remains costlier than common vegetable oils and fats. Richness of milk fat in cholesterol and its association with coronary arterial disease and high blood pressure, combined with modern sedentary life style have compelled people to avoid consumption of food articles and milk products rich in milk fat. There is growing tendency to eat fat free or low fat products as these have significantly low caloric value to enable individuals not to become obese and keep slim-n-trim with body mass index (BMI) within limits. As such several low milk fat and milk fat free "filled" milk and products have emerged.

Filled Milk and Filled Milk Products

Filled milk and milk products contain basically milk ingredients, usually non-fat milk solids and fat other than milk fat. Hedric (1969) referred to filled products as those that replace butter fat in part or in whole by a vegetable fat. However, Fistere (1970) reported that the Federal Filled Milk Act (21, US Code, Section 61-62 of USA in Section

1) defined the term "filled milk", to mean any milk, cream or skimmed milk, whether or not condensed, evaporated, dried to which has been blended with fat or oil other than milk, so that the resultant product is an imitation or resemblance of milk, cream or skim milk whether or not condensed, evaporated, powdered or dried or desiccated. While use of filled milk and products is rapidly increasing in developed countries (Rao, 1985) use of vegetable oil to replace milk-fat in milk and products is not yet permitted (PFA, 1976) in India.

Manufacture of Filled Indian Milk Products

Filled Chhana and Filled Rasogolla

Mandal and Rao (1978) prepared good quality filled chhana from skim milk plus vegetable fat mixture standardized to 5 per cent and 8.5 per cent S.N.F. The mix was tested to 62.5°C, homogenized at 120 kg/cm^2 at the first stage and at 10 kg/cm^2 in the second stage. It was coagulated at 70°C using maida. Filled chhana balls were then cooked in sugar syrup for 15 minutes to yield filled rasgollas. Fifty two percent of the consumers rated the product as good.

Buttermilk as byproduct of butter and ghee industry is available in large quantity in the country. Singh and Ganesh (1988) prepared good quality filled rasogolla using sweet cream buttermilk standardized to 4 per cent fat and 8.5 per cent S.N.F. using skim milk powder and hydrogenated vegetable oil.

Filled channa and good quality of filled rasogolla have also been prepared using 60 per cent buffalo sweet cream buttermilk and 40 per cent of cow milk (3.5 per cent fat) by Bhargava *et al.* (1988). The mixture had 2.0 per cent fat and 8.8 per cent S.N.F.

Acceptability score of rasogolla was found better than those obtained from cow milk with 3.5 per cent fat. Pandey (1984) made good quality sandesh by replacing 60 per cent of cow milk (3.5 per cent fat) with buffalo sweet cream buttermilk.

Soyabean is a rich source of fat good quality protein, vitamins minerals particularly calcium and poor in carbohydrates. Cow milk (2 per cent fat) and buffalo milk (2 per cent fat) when replaced by 20 per cent of soya bean milk, gave rasogolla of acceptable quality (Katara and Bhargava (1994). Any further addition of soyabean milk imparted beany flavour to the product.

Shukla (1989) has also concluded that a mixture either cow cream buttermilk containing 20 per cent cow milk (3.5 per cent fat) can well be replaced upto 20 per cent with reconstituted "Soyal" (soymilk) for production of acceptable quality of rasogolla.

Filled Paneer

Paneer is one of the important indigenous dairy products and is used as a base material for the preparation of a large number of culinary dishes. Buffalo whole milk with 1:1.65 fat and SNF ratio has been recommended for making good quality paneer. This escalates the price of this commodity.

Roy and Singh (1999) attempted to develop filled paneer using skim milk and vegetable oils (Dalda brand vanaspati, groundnut oil and soy oil). The use of domestic mixer as well as centrifugal pump was found satisfactory for mixing milk and oil. However, the use of soy oil resulted in an unacceptable product. Effect of fat level (3.5, 4.5 and 5.5 per cent) revealed that higher the fat level in filled milk, better was the product.

Kheer and Puddings

Kheer is a very popular and delicious cereal based indigenous dessert. Safflower oil is rich in polyunsaturated fatty acids, which help in lowering blood cholesterol and preventing heart disease (Reddy *et al.*, 1993). Narwade *et al.* (2003) found that replacement of buffalo milk with 50 per cent safflower milk gave kheer of acceptable quality with significantly lesser cost and fat content.

Rajadhyax *et al.* (2000) utilized tender coconut with condensed milk for preparation of milk pudding. It was found that mixing 15 per cent of tender coconut milk with condensed milk gave acceptable quality of milk pudding with significantly lower fat content.

Thus filled milk products provide health benefits at lower costs.

Benjamin Franklin invented electricity but the man who innovated the meter now mints money. So let us continue to innovate to benefit the Indian Dairy industry such that better products can be produced at lower cost.

References

Bhargava, V.N., Pandey, V.S., and Shukla, S.G. (1988) Production of Rasogolla from buffalo sweet cream buttermilk fortified with cow milk. Proceedings of the II World Buffalo Congress, Vol. IV 215-224.

Fister, C.M. (1980) Dairy foods and imitations: Legal aspects standards and definitions. Journal of Dairy Science 53(1) 106-108.

Hedrick, T.I. (1969) Imitation and filled products in USA Dairy Industries 34(3), 127-130

Katara, R.V. and Bhargava V.N. (1984) Studies on manufacture of rasogolla from buffalo milk and soya milk blends. Indian Journal of Dairy Science 47(11) 981-986.

Mandal, R.A. and Rao, T.V. (1977) Studies on qualities of filled milk chhana and rasogulla. M.Sc. Thesis, Allahabad University, Allahabad.

Narwade, S.G., Patil, G.R., Sontakke, A.T. and Patil, R.A. (2003) Preparation of kheer from safflower milk blended with Buffalo milk, Indian Journal of Dairy Sciences 56(4)

Pandey, V.S. (1984) Utilization of sweet cream buttermilk for the manufacture of Chhana based seeds. Ph.D. thesis, Banaras Hindu University, Varanasi.

PFA (1976) Prevention of Food Adulteration Act 1976, Ministry of Health and Family Welfare, New Delhi.

Rajadhyax, P., Toro, V.A. and Joshi, S.V. (2000) Utilization of tender coconut for preparation of milk pudding. Indian Journal of Dairy Sciences 53(6) p419-423.

Reddy, S.K., Sharma, K.V. and Reddy, P. (1993) Incorporation of safflower oil in butter to increase PUFA content. Indian Journal of Dairy Sciences 46(8), p375-376.

Roy, S.K. and Singh, S. (1999) Optimization of Processing parameters for manufacture of Paneer from filled milk.; Indian Journal of Dairy Sciences 52(6) p346-351

Shukla, S.G. (1989) Production of chhana and rasogolla from buttermilk fortified with soymilk. Ph.D. thesis, Banaras Hindu University, Varanasi.

Singh, U. and Ganesh (1988) Preparation of filled rasogolla utilizing sweet cream buttermilk solids. Indian Dairyman 40(8) 445-447

Chapter 9

Energy Audit and its Saving in Indian Milk Product Industry

V.N. Bhargava

Retired Professor, A.H. and Dairying, BHU, Varanasi

Director, K.S. Singhal Dairies Pvt Ltd., Agra

Introduction

Energy both thermal and electrical is an important input in dairy manufacturing. Our country is passing through a severe energy crisis and as a result energy is becoming scarce and costly. Sudden increase in costs of fuel and electricity is a matter of great concern today to almost all industries, as it directly affects the production and distribution costs. As neither fuel prices nor electricity tariffs are likely to come down, it is important to audit energy consumption and conserve energy by adopting energy conservation techniques and by generating energy consciousness and awareness amongst the product manufacturing plant employees.

While several case studies on energy audit of milk processing and milk powder making plants (Porwal, 1991, Raychaudhari, 1992, Kjaergaard, 1994, CII 2004) have been done, no report on energy audit in Indian dairy product manufacturing is available. Since the energy conservation measures recommended in the aforesaid studies may also be useful for the Indian milk product plants for energy saving, some of these are stated herein.

Energy Conservation Measures

For Fuel

Significant saving in fuel consumption can be made by adopting correct planning, management and auditing. Some of these are:

Consumption of Fuels

By regulating and periodic monitoring of the various combustion and exhaust gas parameters to optimum levels, combustion efficiency can be improved considerably. Desirable parameters to be maintained for getting maximum combustion efficiency in boiler are:

- ☆ Maximum attainable efficiency: 80-85 per cent
- ☆ CO_2 level in exhaust gases: 12-12.5 per cent
- ☆ Oxygen level: 1-4 per cent
- ☆ Excess Air level: 5-20 per cent
- ☆ Smoke index level: 0-3 Nos.

Cleaning of Fireside

Soot deposition on the fireside reduces rate of heat transfer. Soot deposit of 0.8 mm thickness will result in loss of 9.5 per cent in conductivity and 1.2 per cent drop in boiler efficiency. It is, therefore, essential to keep heat transfer surfaces clean.

Water Side Cleaning

It is said 0.5 mm of scale formation reduces the rate of heat transfer (Verma, 1989). Boiler feed-water hardness should be maintained within permissible limits (less than 5 ppm) by using appropriate water softener and chemical for treating the water. Clean the water softener periodically by resin clean chemicals.

Leakages

Check leakages in steam lines, hot water pipes.

Water Temperature

Control hot water circulation temperature at the pasteurization plant within limits. It should not go too high. For a 10,000 LPH pasteurizer, for each degree rise in temperature, steam consumption increases by 16 kg/hour.

Avoid Idle Running of Boiler

There needs to be a proper coordination with the production department to ensure that there is no idle running of the boiler.

Capacity Utilization

Strive for full capacity utilization of the boiler

Process and System Design

Selection and use of Energy efficient appliances and coil type three pass boiler which minimize energy loss in flue.

Steam

Use dry and low pressure steam. Maintain steam traps, steam control equipment and gauges properly.

Insulation

Have proper insulation of pipes and hot process equipments.

Solar Water

Install solar water heater to preheat boiler feed water to 80°C instead of using it at 25–30°C.

Recovery System

Have a condensate recovery system installed in the plant. Perform regular maintenance tests to ensure recovery system works.

Capacity Boiler

Have proper capacity boiler to match the requirements and have solar water heater for direct use in the pasteurization

Energy Consumption

Energy consumption norms should be formulated for various dairy plant operations.

For Electrical Energy

Electrical energy is mainly used in motors for operating the compressor of the refrigeration plant, milk pumps, water pumps, product processing and packaging systems.

Motor Design

Select motors of proper design according to the parameters found in the dairy. Efficient motors (93 per cent–94 per cent efficiency) are available.

Ice Bank System

The dairy should be designed for peak load but with properly designed ice-bank system. The thumb rule is that for a one lakh LPD capacity diary the coil length in the ice bank system should be 2000 metre.

Insulation

Chilled water pipes should be properly insulated.

Compressor

Have efficient refrigeration compressor. Screw compressors are more efficient.

Scale Formation

Prevent scale formation on condenser pipes. Use softened water for cooling condensers.

Ammonia Compressor Operations

Operate ammonia compressor at suction and head pressure within optimum limits for maximum efficiency.

Capacitors

Install capacitors for low power factor and high efficiency.

Motor Running Schedule

Follow strict schedule for running electric motors.

Repairs and Maintenance

Defects in electric equipment should be promptly attended to. Discard equipment and accessories which cannot be repaired.

Instrumentation and Control System

Proper instrumentation and control system should be installed to ensure that machines are running properly.

Energy Audit

Energy audit should be done periodically.

Proper control over energy expenditure will definitely yield greater profits. Let us disseminate awareness of energy conservation.

References

CII (2004) Detailed Energy Audit of Nestle, India, Moga. Confederation of Indian Industry. Personal communication.

Kjaergaard, G. (1994) Energy efficiency – considerable opportunity for energy saving in the dairy industry. Indian Dairyman 46(9) 563-566.

Porwal, R.K. (1991) Energy conservation in dairy plants – a case study; Indian Dairyman 44(11) 525-529.

Ray Chaudhuri (1992) Conservation of energy in dairy industry and proceedings of the seminar held in Calcutta. Indian Dairyman 44(7) 347-352.

Verma, R.D. (1989) Energy conservation in dairy plants. National workshop on diary plant maintenance and management, No. 2.

Chapter 10

Nutritional Profile Milk and its Product

Indira Bishnoi
Head
Department of Home Science, B.H.U.

Nutrients in Pure Milk

Protein - total	3.2 per cent
Casein protein	2.6 per cent
Whey protein	0.6 per cent
Fat	3.4 per cent
Carbohydrate	4.9 per cent
Water	87 per cent

The above figures are averages only. The composition of milk varies due to different factors such as the breed of cow, feeding, climate, and time of the year.

Vitamins are essential for good health, growth and development. Lack of vitamins can result in deficiency diseases. Milk is a source of many vitamins, including vitamins A, B1, B2, B6, B12, vitamin D and folate. Vitamins A and D are soluble in fat and can be stored in the body. The B vitamins and folate are soluble in water, and as they

Vitamins in Milk

Vitamin	*Role of Vitamin in Human Health*	*Amount in 1 Glass (250mL) of Regular Milk*	*Daily Requirement of an Adult*
A	Healthy skin, eyes and hair; immunity	120 ug	750 ug RE*
B1 - Thiamin	Energy production and growth	0.05 mg	0.8 - 1.1 mg
B2 - Riboflavin	Promotes growth; healthy eyes, hair, skin and nails	0.5 mg	1.2 - 1.7 mg
B6 - Pyridoxine	Essential for protein metabolism; healthy skin, hair and nails	0.15 mg	1.2 - 1.6 mg
B12 - Cyanocobalamin	Growth and maintenance of the nervous system; required for body cell formation and healthy blood	1 ug	2 ug
D	Works together with calcium and phosphorous for healthy bones and teeth	2 ug	No RDI set
Folate (folic acid)	Acts with B12 to assist body cell formation; important before and during early pregnancy	15 ug	200 ug

*RE = retinol equivalents.

Minerals in Milk

Vitamin	*Role of Mineral in Human Health*	*Amount in 1 Glass (250mL) of Regular Milk*	*Daily Requirement– Australian Adult*
Calcium	Maintains strong bones and teeth; regulates nerve and muscle function	295 mg	800 - 1000 mg
Phosphorus	Works with calcium and magnesium to maintain bone structure	232 mg	1000 mg
Magnesium	Maintains bone structure; required for muscle and nerve function	27 mg	270 - 320 mg
Zinc	Important for immunity; healing; reproduction	1 mg	12 mg

are not stored in the body, must be obtained regularly from the foods we eat.

Minerals are nutrients required by humans in small amounts for body metabolism and functions such as body maintenance, structure and regulation. Minerals can't be made in the body and must be obtained from foods we eat.

Milk Composition

Milk is composed of water, carbohydrate (lactose), fat, protein, minerals and vitamins. While each component can be discussed separately, it is important to remember that milk is secreted as a complex mixture of these components. The properties and importance of milk are greater and more complex than the sum of its individual component parts.

Consideration of individual milk components can be viewed from a number of perspectives, including:

- ☆ The biochemistry of each component
- ☆ The mechanisms of synthesis of each component
- ☆ The role of each component in defining the physicochemical properties of milk
- ☆ The function of each component in the mammary gland
- ☆ The importance of each component to the nursing young
- ☆ The importance of each component in milk and milk products as foods for humans
- ☆ The factors which affect variability of milk component composition

Milk Components

Water

Water content of milk is dependent upon the synthesis of lactose. Without some water in the milk, milk would be a viscous secretion composed mostly of lipid and protein and would be extremely difficult to remove from the gland. Upon birth, the mammalian neonate is not able to seek out its own water supply and would dehydrate rapidly without the water component of milk. Water content of milk can range from a low content in marine mammals (see below) to a high content in human milk and others. Cow milk is about 87 per cent water, so the transport of milk from the dairy farm to the processing plant involves hauling considerable amounts of water.

Carbohydrate

Lactose is the *major carbohydrate* in the milk of most species. Lactose is a *disaccharide* composed of the monosaccharides D-glucose and D-galactose, joined in a ß-1,4-glycosidic linkage. The chemical name for lactose is 4-0-ß-D-galactopyranosyl-D-glucopyranose. It is essentially unique to milk, although it has been identified in the fruit of certain plants. Of the mammalian species where information is available, only some marsupials have an alternative sugar other than lactose, and those sugars are generally trisaccharides of glucose and galactose.

Milk Fat

The fat component of milk is composed of a complex mixture of lipids. *Triglycerides* are the major type of lipid in milk fat. Triglycerides are composed of three *fatty acids* covalently bound to a *glycerol* molecule by ester bonds. Milk fat is the major source of lipid used by the neonate mammal for accumulating *body adipose* in the initial days after birth. Most mammalian neonates are born with little body adipose that might be used for insulation or as a source of stored energy. A few days after birth most neonates begin to be able to metabolize milk fat as an *energy source*.

Milk Protein

The total protein component of milk is composed of numerous specific proteins. The primary group of milk proteins are the caseins. There are 3 or 4 caseins in the milk of most species; the different caseins are distinct molecules but have similarities in structure. Caseins have an amino acid composition which is important for growth and development of the nursing young. Caseins are fairly easily digestible in the intestine compared with many other food proteins available. This high quality, easily digestible protein in cow milk is one of the key reasons why milk is such an important human food.

Minerals

The major minerals found in milk are *calcium* and *phosphorous*. These minerals are required in large quantities by the rapidly growing neonate for bone growth and development of soft tissues. They are both mostly associated with the casein micelle structure. Consequently, whey has relatively little calcium and phosphorous compared with whole milk. Milk also contains most other minerals found in the body (see the *Minerals* and *Vitamins* Lesson).

Other Components in Milk

Milk contains all the major vitamins. The fat soluble vitamins A, D, E, and K, are found primarily in the milk fat; milk has only limited amounts of vitamin K. The B vitamins are found in the aqueous phase of milk. Fluid milk in the US is fortified with additional vitamin D. Vitamin A is also added to milk in some other countries.

Physico-chemical Properties of Milk

Milk is an emulsion of fat globules and a suspension of casein micelles (composed of casein, calcium, and phosphorus), all suspended in an aqueous phase which contains solubilized lactose, whey proteins, and some minerals and salts. Leukocytes in milk are part of the suspended phase.

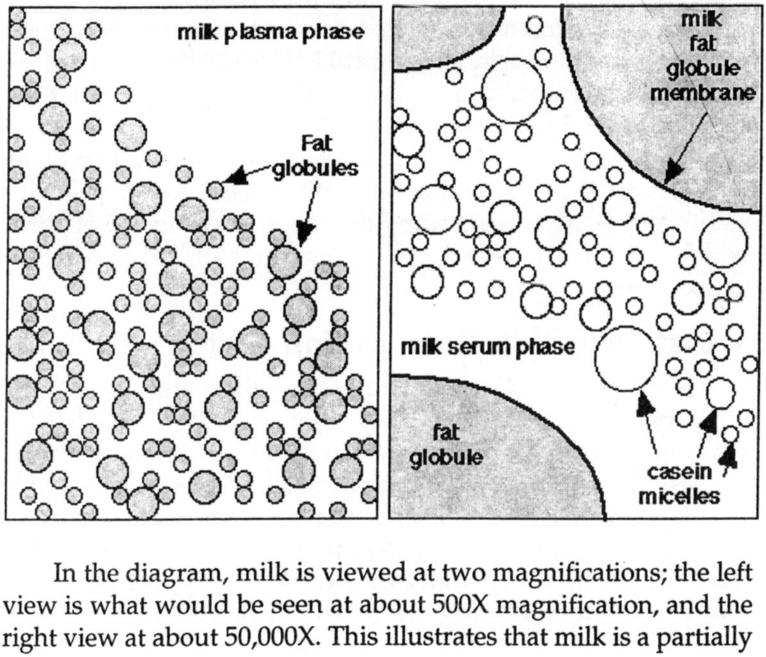

In the diagram, milk is viewed at two magnifications; the left view is what would be seen at about 500X magnification, and the right view at about 50,000X. This illustrates that milk is a partially stable emulsion of milk fat globules (left view) in the plasma phase of milk (the skim milk). In the right view, the casein micelles are in a colloidal suspension in the serum phase of milk (the whey). Milk fat globules in cow milk range in size from 0.1 to 10 micrometers. Milk fat has a density of about 0.92 g/ml. Casein micelles range in size from about 10 to 300 nanometers and have a density of about 1.11 g/ml.

Some other physicochemical characteristics of cow milk include:

- pH of normal milk is about 6.6 - 6.9
- Osmotic pressure is about 700 kPa
- Freezing point depression is about 0.54 K
- Ionic strength is about 0.08 molar
- Water activity is about 0.993

Pasteurization of milk is done to kill bacterial contaminants while not substantially altering the milk characteristics. Heating at 74 C for 15 seconds (low temperature pasteurization) results in killing most organisms and inactivates some enzymes, but does not otherwise alter the milk. Heating at 90 C for 15 seconds (high temperature pasteurization) results in killing all vegetative microorganisms, inactivating most enzymes, but also rendering some whey proteins insoluble. Heating at 118 C for 20 seconds sterilizes the milk, killing all microorganisms, including spores, inactivating all enzyme activities, but also causes changes to the milk such as the browning reaction involving the proteins and sugars. Ultra-high temperature (*UHT*) pasteurization of milk at 145 C for a few seconds sterilizes milk while minimizing the chemical changes. UHT milk which is properly stored has a long shelf life, even at room temperature.

Variation in Milk Composition during a Milking

Even during a milk removal or milking, the composition of milk can vary. Milk fat in the cow provides an example, as indicated in the graph below. Milk fat is lowest in the fore-milk and gradually increases in percentage as the milk is removed. The last milk out of the gland is highest in milk fat content. Somatic cell count (SCC; leukocyte concentration in milk) of milk removed from the gland follows a similar pattern, with the lowest SCC found in the fore-milk (except for the very first few streams of milk removed from the teat)

Transition from Colostrum to Mature Milk in Cows

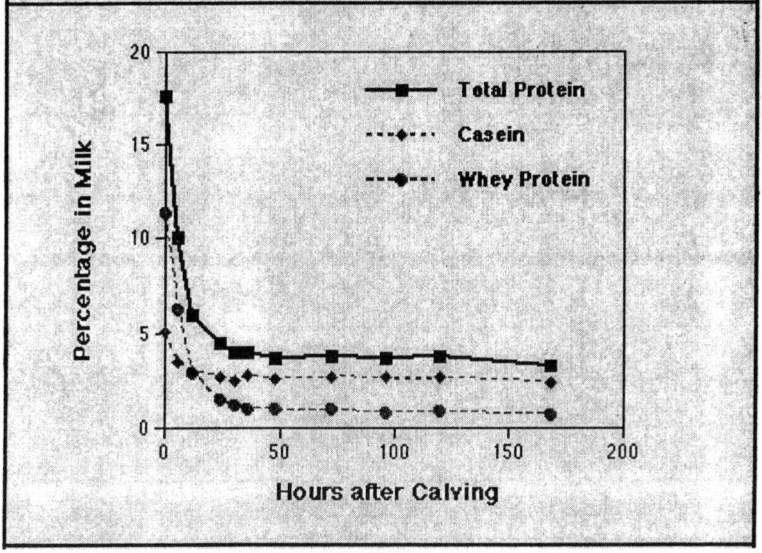

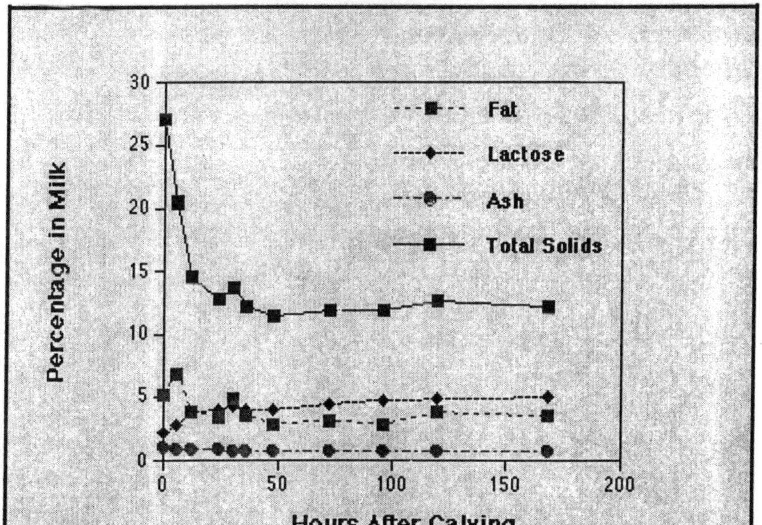

and the highest SCC in the last milk removed from the gland. It is important when taking milk samples from a cow for testing of milk

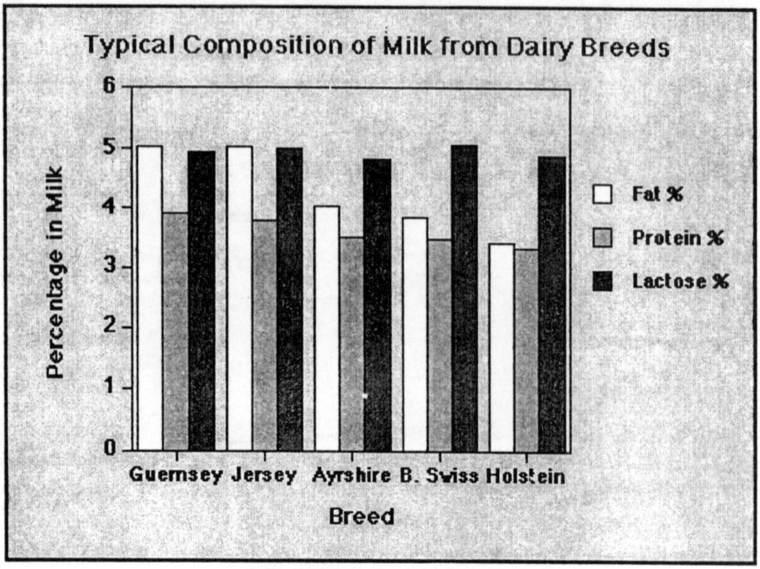

fat and other component that a well mixed sample is taken representing the entire milk collected during a milking.

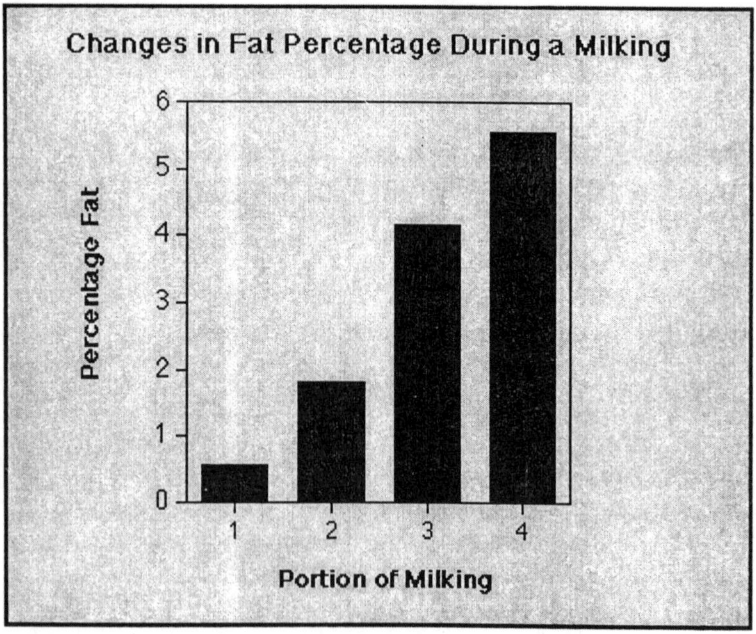

Dairy Product

Dairy products are generally defined as *foodstuffs* produced from *milk*. A production plant for such processing is called a *dairy*. Raw milk for processing generally comes from *cows*, but occasionally from other *mammals* such as *goats, sheep, water buffalo, yaks* or *horses*.

Dairy Farm

There are more than 30 main products made from milk with a number of sub-products in each category. Dairy products include:

- ☆ *Milk*, after optional *homogenization, pasteurization*, in several grades after standardization of the fat level
  - o *Cream*, the fat skimmed off the top of milk or separated by machine-centrifuges
    - § *Sour cream*, cream that has been *fermented* by the bacteria, *Streptococcus lactis* and *Leuconostoc citrovorum*
    - § *Crème fraiche*, slightly fermented cream
  - o *Cultured buttermilk*, fermented concentrated (water removed) buttermilk using the same bacteria as sour cream
  - o *Milk powder* (or powdered milk), produced by removing the water from milk
    - § Whole milk and buttermilk
    - § *Skim* milk
    - § Cream
    - § High milk-fat and nutritional powders (for infant formulas)
    - § Cultured and confectionary powders
  - o *Condensed milk*, milk which has been concentrated by evaporation, often with sugar added for longer life in an opened can
  - o *Evaporated milk*, (less concentrated than condensed) milk without added sugar
  - o *Khoa*

- o *Infant formula,* dried milk powder with specific additives for feeding human infants

☆ *Butter,* mostly milk fat, produced by churning cream

- o *Buttermilk,* the liquid left over after producing butter from cream, often dried as stock food
- o *Butter cream*?
- o *Ghee,* clarified butter, by gentle heating of butter and removal of the solid matter
- o *Anhydrous* milkfat

☆ *Cheese,* produced by coagulating milk, separating from whey and letting it ripen, generally with *bacteria* and sometimes also with certain *molds*

- o *Curds,* the soft curdled part of milk (or skim milk) used to make cheese (or casein)
- o *Whey,* the liquid drained from curds and used for further processing or as a stock food
- o *Cottage cheese*
- o *Cream cheese,* produced by the addition of cream to milk and then cudled to form a rich curd or cheese made from skim milk with cream added to the curd
- o *Fromage frais*

☆ *Casein*

- o *Caseinates*
- o Milk *protein* concentrates and isonates
- o *Whey* protein concentrates and isonates
- o *Hydrolysates*
- o *Mineral* concentrates

☆ *Yoghurt,* milk fermented by *Streptococcus thermophiles* and either *Lactobacillus acidophilus* or *Lactobacillus bulgaricus*

- o *Lassi*

☆ *Gelato,* slowly frozen milk and water

☆ *Ice cream,* slowly frozen cream and emulsifying additives

- *Ice milk*
- *Frozen custard*
- *Frozen yogurt*, yogurt with emulsifiers that is frozen

☆ Other

- *Airag*
- *Kumiss*
- *Viili*
- *Kephir*
- *Filmjölk*
- *Piima*

Dairy Byproducts

Introduction

In recent years there has been wide spread and increasing interest through out the world in creating newer channels of utilization for the by-products of the dairy industry, Conversion of edible substances into non-food items is not ordinarily justifiable especially in countries where there is an overall shortage of milk supplies. It has always been realized that economic disposal of by-products is an essential perquisite to profitable dairying.

Definition

A dairy by-product may be defined as a product of commercial value produced today the manufacture of a main product,

By-Products of Indian Dairy Industry

Main product	*By-product*
Cream	Skim milk
Butter	Butter milk
Ghee	Lassi
	Ghee residue
Chhana/Paneer Cheese Casein	Whey

Composition of Some By-products (Per cent)

Name of By-product (from cow milk)	*Composition*				
	Water	*Fat*	*Protein*	*Lactose*	*Ash*
Skim milk	90.6	0.1	3.6	5.0	0.7
Butter milk (sweet cream)	91.0	0.4	3.4	4.5	0.7
Lassi	96.2	0.8	1.4	1.2	0.4
Ghee residue (sweet-cream butter)	9.7	61.4	24.8	–	4.1
Chhana whey	93.6	0.5	0.4	5.1	0.4
Cheese whey	93.1	0.3	0.9	4.9	0.6
Acid-casein-whey	93.1	0.1	1.0	5.1	0.7

By-products and Names of Food Products Made

By-product	*Food Products Made*
Skim milk	Flavoured milks
	Sterilized flavoured milk
	Cultured butter milk
	Acidophilus milk
	Bulgarian buttermilk
	Concentrated sour skim milk
	Plain condensed skim milk
	Sweetened condensed skim milk
	Low-lactose condensed skim milks
	(Frozen condensed skim milk)
	Dried skim milk
	Cottage cheese/Bakers' cheese/Quarg Gammelost/ Sapsago Casein (edible)
Buttermilk	Condensed buttermilk
Whey	Whey beverage Yeast whey Sweetened condensed milk Whey paste
Lassi	Beverage
Ghee - residue	Toffee or paste

Ghee

Ghee is a clarified butter fat prepared from cow or buffalo milk. The largest ghee producing states are U.P., A.P, Punjab, Rajasthan, M.P., Bihar, Haryana etc. The production of ghee is higher in winter and lower in summer.

Method of Preparation

Cream accumulated after few days is usually taken in 3 suitable vessel and heated and stirred on a low flame to remove the moisture contain. After removing moisture contain further heating is stopped then cooling is done. On cooling, when the residue has settled down the clear fat is decanted into suitable containers.

Characteristics	*Cow*	*Buffalo*
Milk fat	99 to 99,5%	
Moisture	Not more than 0.5%	
Uneaponiable matter		
Carotene (m g./g.)	3.2-7.4	-
VIt.A (I.U./g.)	19-34	17-38
Charred casein, salls of copper and iron, etc.	Max.2.8 (Agmark)	Traces

Lassi

Lassi, also called chhas or matha, refers to desi buttermilk, which is the by-product obtained when churning curdled whole milk with crude indigenous devices for the production of desi butter (makkhan). It appears that 50-60 kg. (ave.55kg) of lassi are produced for every kg of ghee. Lassi contains appreciable amounts of milk proteins and phospholipids.

Composition

Characteristics	*Milk (Per cent)*	*Characteristics*	*Milk (Per cent)*
Water	96.2	Total solids	3.8
Fat	0.8	Solids-not-fat	3.0
Protein	1.3	Lactose	1.2
Ash	0.4	Lactic acid	0.44

Buttermilk

Condensed Buttermilk

Also known as semi-solid buttermilk, this is usually sweet cream buttermilk which has been ripened and condensed (approx, 3 : 1) in much the same way as concentrated sour skim milk. Alternatively, sour-cream buttermilk may be used without ripening it, but the acidity (lactic) of the buttermilk prior to its being condensed should be greater than 1.6 per cent. This will ensure in the finished product a 5–6 per cent acidity, which is necessary for long keeping quality. Either sour whey or an organic acid (such as lactic, acetic, citric or tartaric) may be used to increase the acidity of buttermilk.

Dairy Buttermilk

Soft Cheese from Buttermilk

The production of soft cheese from creamery buttermilk may be outlined as follows; fresh buttermilk, obtained by churning sweet-cream butter, is admixed with fresh skim milk in the proportion of 1:1. The mixture is pasteurized at 65°C for 20 minutes, cooled to 35°C, inoculated with lactic starter @ 10 per cent and allowed setting for 3 hours. The curd is cut with standard cheese knives and the curd cubes subjected to a cooking process during which a maximum of 40°C is reached in 15-20 minutes. The curd cubes are then collected in a muslin cloth and pressed overnight, preferably inside cold store (5-10°C), to remove excess moisture. The pressed curd, which has a rather low keeping quality, can be utilized either for direct consumption after the addition of sugar @ 15 per cent, or in the manufacture of processed cheese up to 10 per cent of raw cheese.

India's Traditional Dairy Products

From burfi to kulfi, from *kalakand* to *ŝhrikhand*, from *gulabjamun* to *chumchum* extends the delectable world of Indian *milk delicacies*.This article brings together information culled from diverse sources on age-old, milk-based specialties from different regions. Also included is information culled from diverse sources on the Indian milk-based sweets and other specialties from different regions of the country.

Curd

The first of these products developed was *dahi* (curds or yogurt), obtained by fermenting milk. In the process, the digestibility of milk constituents improves.The product is widely consumed along with meals. The surplus dahi is used as the intermediate product and churned into *makkhan* (butter), while the liquid whey — *chhach* or *mattha* — is consumed as a refreshing beverage or converted into *kadhi*, a spicy dish served hot with rice.

Nutritional benefits: When food is supplemented with 250 gms of dahi a day, the status of thiamine improves. *Dahi* also increases the pyruvic and lactic acids among children on a typical poor rice diet. Due to fermentation of milk, a greater amount of phosphorus and calcium is made available to the digestive system by their precipitation in the lower intestines due to the acid condition induced by *Lactobacillus* sp. The consumption of sour milk also results in increased efficiency of the human body to cope with a sudden influx of lactic acid in the system. Dahi can also be consumed by people who suffer from lactose intolerance. Thus, dahi in its different forms as lassi, kadhi, shrikhand, etc. also contributes significantly to improve the nutritive contents of an average Indian diet.

Ghee and Makkhan

A week's collection of makkhan(butter) is converted into *ghee*. *Dahi* has a shelf-life of a day or two; *makkhan*, a week; and *ghee*, about a year. Ghee, thus, became the main dairy product for extended preservation. A system of collection of ghee from villages for trade gradually developed. Ghee mandis (trading centers) have been in existence for centuries. India produces some 900,000 tonnes of *ghee*, valued at Rs 85,000 million.The value of the resultant *lassi* is Rs 25,000 million.

Butter-milk is a by-product in the preparation of *makkhan*. It is estimated that about 55 kg of butter-milk is produced for every kg of ghee. While most of it is consumed by villagers and their families, some quantity is either given away or fed to cattle. The reason for this is lack of any market for it in rural areas. Butter-milk is rich in milk protein and calcium, and forms a nutritive and refreshing beverage.

Khoa and Chhana

One major milk product in common use is *khoa*, obtained by rapidly evaporating milk in shallow pans to a total solids of about 70 per cent and capable of being preserved as such for several days.

It is used as an ingredient in making different kinds of traditional mithais (sweets) such as *peda, burfi* and *gulabjamun*. Some 900,000 tonnes of khoa valued at Rs 45,000 million is produced in the country.

Yet another milk product of significance is *chhana*, a product of acid coagulation of hot milk and draining out of whey. It is used in preparing different kinds of sweets such as rasagollas. As they are especially popular in the Eastern region, they are called Bengali sweets. Approximately 1,200,000 tonnes of chhana, valued at Rs 6,000 million is produced in India.

Chapter 11

Impact of Animal Health on the Quality of Milk and Dairy Products

H.N. Singh, S.D. Sharma and Sharad Kumar Singh

U.P. Pt. D.D.U. Pashu Chikitsha Viswa Vidyalaya Evam Go Anusdhan Santhan, Mathura, U.P.

Animal produces particularly milk has an important role in livestock economy not only for the producer but also for the country. The important task for veterinarian is continuous improvement of efficiency of livestock production by management of animal health. Besides, nutrition, breeding and general management practices of milk producing animals, economical methods of diseases diagnosis and treatment, monitoring animal health and production, specific disease prevention and control programs (vaccination, deworming) and promoting management practices to ensure milk supply free of biological and chemical agents, all are important facts, where veterinary expertise is of outmost importance not only to enhance the existing milk production but also quality of milk and milk products production, as is envisaged in the national plan for global competition. Diseases not only affect the quantity but also quality (change in chemical composition in particular) of milk and may even pose risk of transmission of infection or drug-residues to human society.

Some of the important disease/ailments, which affect milk production both quantity and quality are as under:

Udder Diseases

Bovine udder is involved many a times to risk of injury (wound, cracks) and diseases like mastitis, blood in milk, udder edema, impetigo etc. Mastitis alone is causing a loss amounting approximately Rs.6000 crores per annum in the country. A sub clinical mastitis whose incidence is much more than the clinical mastitis, is of special concern. Proper management practices particularity udder hygiene, regular milk examination by platform test and timely therapy based on sensitivity results and culling of chronic cases are important steps in curtailing losses due to these udder problem. Proper milking technique, sanitation of cow, its byre and udder/teats particularly pre and post partum care and miscellaneous care *e.g.* Nutrition, housing, management of teat lesions, fly control and disinfect ion of gwala¢s hands are important in the control programme.

Gastrointestinal Parasitism

Various epidemiological surveys have established the permanent prevalence of helminthes in animals, which are important in reducing the productivity. Fasciola in liver, Amphistoma in rumen, and Bursate worms (*Haemonchus, Ostertagia, Cooperia, Nematodirus, Trichostrongylus* sp.) in G.I.T. all are important in producing animals. Good plane of nutrition (Cobalt, Copper, Phosphorus and Protein deficient in particular reducing animals resistance), pasture management (rotational grazing, set stocking, zero grazing, drainage, fencing), vector control (snails, beetles, insects), regular deworming with suitable anthelmintic (Protective dosing twice/thrice a year), Excreta disposal, avoidance of interspecies transmission, are all important steps in keeping a check over the parasitism to a level with little or no harm with regard to milk production.

Haemoprotozoa

Babesiosis, Anaplasmosis, trypanosomiasis, Theleriosis in particular are of major concern in producing animals, as well there are transmitted by insect vectors (Ticks and Flies) which are quite prevalent all over the country. These disease affect production in both ways *i.e.* mortality as well as high morbidity risk. Subclinical infection is not uncommon. The risk factors are susceptible to infection (crossbred and exotic being at great risk) climate and environment (temperature, humidity, rainfall affecting vector-activity), case of transmission (rapid and continuous transmission by vector and its stages) and premunity.

Regular survellence, prophylactic and curative treatment, immunotherapy (theileriosis) and vector control are important in curtailing the economic constraint due to these diseases.

Production/Metabolic Diseases

In milk producing cows and buffaloes a number of important metabolic disease affect their milk productions a lot. Usually these diseases are the result of an imbalance between rates of input and output of dietary nutrients. Postparturent paresis, Acetonemia, hypoglycemic therapy tetany, post parturient haemoglobinuria (PPH-Hypophosphataemia), Downers Cow Syndrome, Fatty Liver Diesases, Low milk fat syndrome are some important production diseases of cows and buffaloes.

Analysis of feed, fodder and soil and use of metabolic profile tests (Blood profile), milk estimation, average daily food intake etc) are to be employed on herd basis (a village may be a unit) for the production of these diseases and accordingly energy requirement specific dietary demands of the producing animals may be met with for the control of production diseases in form animals, besides improvement in management practices (pre and post partum case, acute weather management).

Dietary Mineral/Vitamin Deficiencies

Farming practices and lack of veterinary counseling have marked bearing on presence or absence of specific dietary nutrients. Intensive use of nitrogen fertilizers to soil reduces, copper, cobalt, molybdenum and manganese content of pasture. Application of lime reduces Cu. Co, Zn, Mn but increase Mo-content. Absorption in intensive is important. Excess of phosphate reduces Ca-absorption; excess of Ca reduces absorption of iodine, fluorine, lead, Zinc of Cadmium. Hay making though conserve vitamin A but reduces Vitamin D. green feed in availability during pregnancy causes hypo vitaminosis-A. These dietary deficits not only causes production losses through various mechanisms but also incline the animal to become picatic which is more dangerous state affects quality of milk in turn. Knowledge of local forming of feeding practices is thus of utmost importance in the diagnosis of management of nutritional deficiency states. vitaminA and E, micro minerals like Cu, Co and Zinc are now being recommended for nutritional therapy in many a diseases as they are found decreased in diseases pathogens. Even single sodium chloride deficiency is likely to occur under hot environmental conditions, grazing over pasture on sandy soils, heavily fertilized with potash and during lactation period.

Antibiotic Residues in Milk

A number of antimicrobial are frequently use for treatment of animal diseases. Antibiotic contamination of milk posses a public health risk and also may cause problem in manufacture of milk products such as affect on starter culture for chees and yoghurt can result in total loss of large amount of manufacturing milk.A withholding period for sale market milk is necessary in antibiotic treated animal. Sulphonamide, Tetracyclins, penicillin, Aminoglycocydes, Cephalosporin and chloramphenicol, have all been detected in milk. Milk testing system for antibiotic residues at frequent interval should be adopted for safety reasons. Use of only approved antimicrobials at label dose, should be done to minimize the possibility of antibiotic residues in milk.

Chapter 12

Ghee: Legal Standards, Validity and Limitation to Detect Adultration

Jagdish Prasad

Dean, F/o, Veterinary Science and Animal Husbandry
Allahabad Agricultural Institute-Deemed University,
Allahabad, U.P.

Ghee is a clarified butter fat prepared cow or buffalo milk. An average ghee sample has more than 99.5 milk fat and remaining includes moisture and very small amount of milk solids not fat and associated extraneous matter. A good ghee has its characteristic aroma, flavour, and taste, which are essential attributes for consumers' acceptance. A good ghee should have well developed granules dispersed fairly thickly and uniform over the entire mass. Typical ghee has following composition.

Ingredients	*Cow Milk Ghee*	*Buffalo Ghee*
Milk fat per cent	99 – 99.5	99 – 99.5
Moisture per cent	0.2 – 0.5	0.2 – 0.5
Carotene mg/g	3.2 – 7.4	–
Vit. A 11/g	19 – 34	17 – 38
Tocopherol mg/g	26 – 48	18 – 37
Free fatty acid (per cent oleic)	1.3	1.3

Legal Requirements for Export of Ghee in India

Butyrorefrectometer reading at 40°	:	40–45
R.M. value	:	21–28
Free fatty acid per cent Oleic (max.)	:	3.0
Moisture (max.) per cent	:	0.5

Therapeutic Value

Ghee contains about 5 times the level of conjugated linoliec acid (CLA) than that is present in original milk fat. CLA is known to be anti-carcinogenic agent, also known as anti-oxidant contributing to long keeping quality of ghee at ambient temperature. It also supplies Vitamin A, D, E and K.

Validly and Limitation

To protect consumers interest and duck adulteration the govt. has fixed legal standards for ghee. The market receives ghee with high moisture and or with high acidity. Both these affect the keeping quality.

Cause of Adulteration

(i) limited availability of milk, production of ghee is not commensurate with demand. This leads to adulteration on a fairly large scale, with animal fat or vanaspati; (ii) another reason is to improve the quality substandard ghee by fraudulent practices. (iii) Ghee being most expensive of fats, becomes easy prey to admixture with cheap adulterants by middlemen.

Limitations

Food laws are sufficiently comprehensive, application of laws become inefficient due to easy, quick and fool proof method of detection of adulteration. For various reasons presumptive tests are of limited value. It is only in this context seasonal Boudoir test has been devised to detect adulteration of ghee with Vanaspati. All Vanaspati manufacturers should add 1 per cent sesame oil before final packing so that it can be detected by simple test; has been mandatory.

Use of Corrected B.R.

B.R. reading decreases and increased with a rise and fall, respectively, in temperature. Normally temperature of observation should not deviate by more than ± 2°C. However, if temperature is not exactly at 40°C then 0.55 is added to the observed B.R. reading for each degree above 40°C. After temperature correction (if any) no further correction is needed. However, in case of fat isolation by the modified Gerber method, the B.R. readings are suppressed probably due to inherent hydraulic effect of H_2SO_4 on the fat. Therefore, in such care observed (o) B.R. be corrected as follows:

CBR = 0BR + (0.08 x BR)

B.R. reading of clear milk fat should be constant with value given for ghee under PFA rules, 1955. Any deviation from the standard from the standard values shall indicate adulteration.

This method has limitation in detection of milk fat adulteration by two oils, *i.e.* Coconut oil and palm oil whose B.R. values are close to that of milk fat.

Problems of Adulteration

Main Adulterants of Ghee

1. Vanaspati (hydrogenated vegetable oil)
2. Refined (de-odourized) vegetable oil.
3. Animal body fat
4. Miscellaneous, plant in rice, potato etc.

Stages of Adulteration

Production, assemblage and marketing – the last one is crucial at which max. adulteration takes place.

Reasons for Giving Room for Adulteration

1. Lack of well organized system of food inspection.
2. Lack of availability of laboratory facilities.
3. Absence of easy method for detection of adulteration.

Govt. Law for Compulsory Addition of Sesame Oil

1. Indian Govt. has made compulsory that all Vanaspati must contain a max. 5 per cent of sesame oil, so that it may be detected by simple Boudoir test. Adulteration of ghee with Vanaspati to an extent as low as 3 per cent can be detected.

2. Possibility of use of colour: Pink extract of rattan jot (*Onusma echioides*), extract of chlorophyll, Turmeric are be tried to give different colour to Vanaspati for easy detection but still satisfactory colour is get to be evolved.

AGMARK Standards for Ghee

Sl.No.	*Tests*	*All India*	*Regional*	
			Winter	*Summer*
1.	Boudoir		Negative	
2.	Phytosterol acetate		Negative	
3.	BR at 40ºC	40–30	41.5–44	42.5–45
4.	RM Value	Not less than 28.0	Not less than 23.0	Not below 21.0
5.	P. value	1.1–2.0	0.5–1.2	0.5–1.0
6.	Moisture per cent not more than 3%			
7.	Free fatty acid (Percent oleic)			
8.	a) Special grade tot more than 1.4%			
	b) General grade not more than 2.5%			

Source: Indian Dairyman. 28(7) 219 (1976).

Limitations

1. Absence of quality consciousness on part of producers and consumers.
2. Absence of organolaptic quality standards.
3. Region-wise variation natural quality and difficulty in meeting Indian consumers acceptability in accordance with AGMARK Packers.

References

Anankrishnan, CP; Khan, AQ and Padmanabhan, PN 1994. Milk product preparation and quality control. Shri Laxmi Pub. Madras, 233-236.

Arora, K.L., Lal, D., Seth, R. and Ram, J. 1996. Plot form test for detection of refined mustard oil adulteration in milk. *Indian J. Dairy Sci.* 49(10): 721-723.

Bodhe, AM 1988. Detection of Adulteration in Milk. Indian Dairyman 50(7): 16-18.

De, S. 1988. Outlines of Dairy Technology. Oxford University Press, Delhi, Fourth Ed. Pp. 426-462.

Dastur, NN; Kannan, A. and Kothawala, ZR. 1947. *Ind. J. Vet. Sci.* 17(3): 171.

I.S. 3508, 1966. Methods of sampling and test for ghee (butter fat). Bureau of Indian Standards, Manak Bhawan, New Delhi.

Ramamurthy, MK; Narayanan, KM, Bhalerao, VR. And Dastur, NN. 1967. *Ind. J. Dairy Sci.* 20(1): 11.

Rangappa and Achanja 1974. *Indian Dairy Products.*

Srinivasan, MR. 1976. Indian Dairyman, 28(7): 279.

Singhal, PP. 1980. Adulteration and Methods for detection. Indian Dairyman, 32: 771-774.

SP: 18 (Part XI) (1981). Handbook of food Analysis Part XI. Dairy Products. BIS. Manak Bhawan, New Delhi.

Chapter 13

Therapeutic Use of Milk and Milk Products

Jagdish Prasad
Dean, Faculty of Veterinary Science and Animal Husbandry, Allahabad Agricultural Institute-Deemed University, Allahabad – 211 007, U.P.

In the developing countries which are economically backward malnutrition prevails on account of the fact that the population by and large can ill afford expensive easily digestible protein rich food of animal origin. This situation in countries like India is further complicated because majority of its on account of religious prejudices vegetarians abhor protein of animal origin except milk because it is considered a product of ahimsa. Even the cost of milk is high and few of the people can ill afford to drink in quantities considered necessary.

Drink Milk its Could Save Your Life (Brody, 2003)

Researchers from Cincinnati Children's Hospital through American Journal of Clinical Nutrition of Jan 2003, reported that adult women who consumed less than a glass of milk a day during childhood had flimsier bones and a two-fold risk of fractures than those who consumed a glass of milk or more each day.

Some people avoid milk because they are lactose-intolerant and experience flatulence/diarrhoea when drinking milk on an empty stomach. Nutrition however have found that most lactose – intolerant people can handle.

Milk: A Nutritious and Protective Food

Milk occupies a unique position among foods, being complete food for infants, good supplementary food for people of all ages and essential protective food for sick and invalids. Milk proteins are highly nutritious that effectively supplements poor quality vegetable proteins in a mixed diet. Milk proteins and peptides have several therapeutic and prophylactic properties and protect against gastrointestinal disorders, hypertension and enteric infection. Milk is a rich source of all vitamins especially Vitamin A, riboflavin and Vitamin B_{12}. Milk is a richest natural source of calcium in the best available form. Milk contains several extranutritional constituents such as conjugated linoleic acid spingomylins, butyric acid, myristic acid and β-carotenes, which protect against cancer, cardiovascular diseases, enteric injection and diabetes, besides having immunomodulatory and slimming effect. Mother's milk contains large amount of several antimicrobial substances such as immunoglobins, lactoferrin, lysozyme, lactoperoxidase and vitamin B_{12} binding protein that protect infants against enteric injection. Milk contain serum cholesterol lower factors. Lactic acid produced from milk sugar, lactose, inhibit the growth of proteolytic and putrefying bacteria in the large intestine. There is no scientific base for implicating milk in cardiovascular disease, diabetes, cancer etc; all such concerns are unfounded (Kansal, 2004).

Therapeutic Properties of Different Milks

Camel Milk

Mal *et al.* (2004) conducted a study to determine therapeutic efficacy of Camel milk on human patients affected with tuberculosis (TB) in the dept. of TB and Chest diseases of S.P. Medical College Bikaner. The patients were grouped as G_1 (empyema) and fresh pulmonary T.B. (G2) having a control group in each. The patients were given standard therapy along with raw milk @ 1 kg/day as supplement. The clinical symptoms, bacteriological, radiological, haemotological and biochemical parameters were recorded at monthly intervals. However, body weight was recorded fortnightly.

Results revealed that at the end of trial increase in appetite, no pus formation, more radiological improvement in terms of lung expansions was found in patients kept on Camel milk supplement in G_1. Haematological parameters showed significantly higher haemoglobin (P <0.01, significant reduction in neutrophils in patients of empyuma TB supplemented with Camel milk. The activity of LDM (Lactate dehydrogenase was significantly lower (P< 0.05) in patients fed with Camel milk in G1, while zinc was significantly higher (P<0.01). Increase in body weight was also seen. Increase in appetite, reduction in radiological reflections, significantly higher (P<0.05), haemoglobin content, reduction ESR and TLC (P<0.05) was noticed in patients with fresh pulmonary T.B. receiving Camel milk (G_2). Significantly higher (P<0.05) in body weight were found in the patients whose diet had been supplemented with Camel milk. It means that Camel milk can out as adjuvant nutritional supplement.

Goat Milk

1. Goat milk has relatively higher content of vit. B and helpful in relieving symptoms of 'stress', neutrotic indigestion and constipation.
2. It is an Ayurvedic medicine for persons ailing with asthma cough and sugar troubles.
3. Has higher buffering qualities which enhances its value for those suffering from peptic ulcer and digestive troubles requiring treatment with anti-drugs.
4. Being higher in Phosphorus prevents Phosphorus deficiency in vegetarians.
5. Has less allergic problems rather very rare than other milk. (Internet news).
6. Provides better nutrition than other livestock species for human and hence "foster mother" for man.
7. Its milk being alkaline has medicinal value and recommended from pyloric stenosis, alyspepsia, peptic ulcer, allergic eczema and infantile diarrhoea. Its milk has therapeutic value in liver disfunction, jaundice, biliary disorder, acidosis and insomia.
8. Goat milk is lower in chlolesterol and higher in Ca, P and Vita A and B.

9. Cow milk takes for digestion one day but goats milk is digested in 20 minutes.

Role of Milk and Milk Products in Relation to Health and Diseases (Gupta, 2003)

Milk contain all the constituents like high quality protein, easily digestible fat, bone and teeth forming calcium and phosphorus and essential life giving vitamins.

Milk Proteins

Milk proteins consist of all essential amino acids, hence have a very high NPU of 83. Casein is the major protein that constitutes about 80 per cent of the total protein. Another class of protein namely minor milk proteins which is derived from whey is referred to as whey proteins. These proteins possess high concentration of sulphur containing amino acids and are easily digestible. Because of their low phenylalanine and tyrosine content, they find use in dietetic food formulations for patients suffering from disease like phenylketo urea, tyrosenemia and hyper phenylallaninemia. These proteins have the capacity to associate with vitamins and facilitate the transfer of vitamins to different tissues of the body.

Milk contains some protective like Leucocytes, antibodies, Lysozymes, Lactoferin, Lactoperoxidase, Xanthine oxidase and immuno-globulins which inhibit a wide range of bacteria. Milk derived peptides play an important bacteria. Milk derived peptides play an important role in controlling metabolic processes like digestion, circulations, immunolygical responsiveness, cell growth, repair and nutrient intake.

Milk Lipids

Fat is utilized mainly as a source of energy. Milk fat consists primarily of triglycerides with small amount of di-and mono-glycerides, phospholipids, sterole, carotenoids, fat soluble vitamins and some traces of free fatty acids. The fatty acid composition of milk fat is characterized by a high proportion of saturated fatty acids (25-30 per cent) and small amount of polysaturated fatty acids (4 per cent) some beneficial effects of milk fat are:

1. Efficient digestion and absorption as it contains a high proportion of short and medium chain fatty acids which

are digested and absorbed by the body more efficiently than the longer chain fatty acids.

2. Antibacterial properties of fatty acids especially those of short and medium chain length. They inhibit the activity of microbes in the alternative tract.
3. Protective effect on teeth.
4. Anti-cancer effect.
5. Cholesterol lowering effect.
6. Others *e.g.* it provides body with essential fatty acids like linoleic and linoleic acids, phosphlipids exert a protective effect on lining of stomach etc.

Milk Corbohydrate

The major carbohydrate of milk is lactose which varies from 4.4 to 5.2 per cent in bovine milk. The various functions of lactose in the body are to provide energy, inhibit putrefaction by promoting the growth of aciduric bacteria in the intestine, facilitate the absorption of minerals like calcium, magnesium, zinc and phosphorus and to develop of the infant's brain.

Milk Minerals

Milk is good source of sodium, potassium, chloride, calcium, phosphorus and magnesium. Some specific functions of milk minerals are:

1. Sodium is a principle cation is the regulation of Osmolarity, acid base balance and active transport across the cell membranes.
2. Chloride is an essential cellular anion for the maintained of fluid and electolyte balance.
3. Potassium a principal intercellular cation that controls muscular activities and blood pressure.
4. Calcium is important from health and nutrition point of view as it plays a beneficial role in controlling Osteoporosis, hypertension and protects against color cancer and helps in controlling blood lipid level.

Milk Vitamins

Milk is an important dietary source of various vitamins and it is one of the excellent source of riboflavin which is necessary for growth, proper functioning of eyes and lining of the mouth and lips and prevention of premature aging of the skin. For vegetarian people milk is the only source of Vitamin B_{12} which is required for the maturation of RBCs in the body and it's deficiency result in a disease known as Pernicious anaemia. Also, milk is a good source of fat soluble vitamins.

Milk and Milk Products in Health Care

Milk and Milk Products in Relation to Cardiovascular Diseases

Milk and its products make a relatively small contribution to total fat and cholesterol intake as compared to fats and oils, meat, poultry and fish. Saturated fatty acid (SFA) intake is one of the strongest predicators of blood cholesterol levels. Although milk fat is important source of SFAs, its content of stearic-acid and short and medium chain fatty acids minimize the expected increase to other saturated fats.

Makhal *et al.* (2004) reported that according to our traditional antique practices, the intake of natural and unprocessed ghee and makhan also prop up their multipurpose medicinal value rather than their unauthentic hyperholesterolemic type. When milk and milk products are consumed in usual amounts, they don't appear to adversely influence the blood lipid levels or augment the CHD (Coronary heart Disease) risk. Several experiments with volunteers have shown that blood cholesterol level does not rise even when as much as two litre of milk is consumed daily.

Recent scientific findings with milk fat in relation to its multipurpose medicinal value have also supported the benefits of intake of natural and unprocessed ghee and butter, rather than their unauthentic hypercholesterolemic hype, which have been practised in our traditional culture since the age as depicted in our ancient testaments. Milk fat present in dairy products becomes an essential component due to its high nutritional biochemical properties. Its biological significance is determined by cholesterol reducing ability, anticarcinogenic properties, etc.

Hypocholesterolemic Effect

Milk and milk products (Yoghurt, acidophilous milk) lower serum cholesterol levels in human both by decreased formation and increased breakdown of cholesterol by bile acids in liver. Orotic acid present in milk has cholesterol reducing property.

Milk and Milk Products in Oral Health

Milk and milk products as rich source of calcium, phosphorus, magnesium, fluoride and trace minerals play important role in the development of oral tissues. Milk products like cheddar and Swiss cheese have protective properties and inhibit caries formation.

Milk and Milk Products in Hypertension

Available Scientific evidence indicates that adequate intake of calcium, potassium and magnesium, all the three found in milk and milk products has a positive effect on the blood pressure. Milk products like yoghurt, skim and low fat milk lower the risk of hypertension.

Milk and Milk Products in Osteoporosis

Milk and milk products such as whole milk, cheese and youghut are the major sources of calcium in a vegetarian diet. Increasing dietary intake of Ca and Vit. D by consuming more serving of dairy foods not only is beneficial to bone health but it is relatively safe.

Milk and Milk Products in Cancer

Milk protein (Casein) is very efficient antimutagenic agent. Casein on enzymatic hydrolysis gives peptides which have immunostimulatory properties. These immunopeptides stimulate phagocytic activity of human peripheral lymphocytes.

Similarly whey proteins also release some peptides and amino acids during digestion which may stimulate antibody production and the process of phagocytosis. Another important whey protein, lactoferrin also has a great potential in treatment of cancer.

Chicks on Milk to Reduce Digestibility Problems

Milk products have a positive effect on the performance and health of chickens. Nutrified of Veghel in the Netherlands developed a new concept for feeding young chickens based on milk products.

For decades, farmers have been using milk ingredients on top of poultry feed. They use milk ingredients when the animals are under stress or when the birds have problems with digestibility.

During the eighties, it was even compulsory in the EV to use milk powder in poultry and pig rations to get rid of the enormous amount of milk powder that was stocked for intervention. When using milk ingredients, the farmers see an increase in performance and health.

Nutrified developed a product based on milk ingredients combined with specific emulsifiers to increase the fat digestibility and the health status of animal.

This feeding concept is called Avilac, was also nominated for an innovation Award.

Enzyme lipase is increased and the less absorptive fatty acids are more easily absorbed through the use of emulsifiers. The result of this is an increase in the fat digestibility.

However, there are indications that besides the effect on fat digestibility, the digestibility of carbohydrates is also improved.

Milk ingredients do have a prebiotic effect on the microflora of the animal. The milk ingredients are used as a substrate by Lactobacilli and Bifido spp.

The results of this is an increase in volatile fatty acids (VFA). These VFAs have an anti-bacterial effect in the gastrointestinal tract, and increase the competitive exclusion.

This leads to an improved intestinal health and, as a result, less gastrointestinal lesions and diseases (gastro-enteritis).

Table 13.1: Performance of Broilers Fed with a Commercial Diet and a Diet with Avilac

Trial a	*Control 0.5 per cent N=20,000*	*Avilac HB N=30,000*
Daily gain (q/day))	47.62	49.43
FCR*	1.759	1.642
Body wt. (g)	2000	2026
Mortality per cent	4.9	3.2
Trial b	N= 19500	N = 33000
Dairy gain (q/day)	45.88	47.01
FCR*	1.6542	1.612
Body wt. (g)	20061	2142
Mortality per cent	4.2	2.8

* Feed conversion ratio re-calculated to weight of **1500 g**.

Probiotic Cultures in Dairy Foods (Sabikhi and Mathur, 2010)

Probiotic cultures contribute towards a better gastrointestinal environment in man or animal, thus improving the genetic health and well-being. They strengthen the immune system, protect against infections, constipation and diarrhoeal disorders, breakdown carcinogenic substances, lower serum cholesterol level, reduce the incidence of intestinal tumours, metabolise lactose and reduce lactose intolerance, improve absorption of calcium, aid in the treatment of peptic ulcer, synthesise vitamins and predigest proteins. There has been a phenomenal growth of foods containing these probiotic cultures, particularly in western Europe, USA and Japan. The most prominent among these products are acidophilus bifidus yoghurt and bifidus milk, with a recent interest in probiotic cheese varieties. The major technological challenges in the manufacture of probiotic dairy foods are the selection of strains that can withstand the rigorous conditions of processing and storage of the product, and are able to survive in adequate numbers in the product, besides being tolerant to the low pH and high bile concentration in the upper digestive tract.

Limitations

It is always said that milk is a balanced package of nutrients having all in one although it has some limitations, which may pose problems in certain cases.

Lack in Nutrients

Milk cannot serve as source of some nutrients like copper, Iron and Vitamin C.

Lactose Intolerance

Some infants and even adults are not able to tolerate milk, but can assimilate dahi. This is primarily due to lactose in tolerance. These subjects suffer from an inherent deficiency in the intestinal enzyme called lactase (b-D-galactosidase) which is responsible to cleave lactose to glucose and galactose.

Milk Allergies

The milk protein, as a cause of allergy have been reported in some cases.

Galacosemia

In this hereditary disease, the individual is unable to metabolize galactose because of deficiency of an enzyme uridyltransferase which converts galactose into glucose. As a result galactose accumulates in the body causing cataract, liver and kidney malfunction and brain damage.

Coronary Heart Diseases

Milk contains both saturated fat and cholesterol level and increased cholesterol levels are believed to play an important role in development of heart diseases.

Kidney Stones

Milk is a rich source of calcium. Excessive calcium intake is associated biochemically with a rise in blood calcium (hypercalcemia) and/or with a significant increase in urinary calcium (hypercalciuria) and other adverse symptoms of calcium excess may include renal failure, soft tissue calcification, irritability and headache. High calcium intake might also be associated with an increase risk of kidney stone formation in susceptible individuals.

Milk Microbes

Milk is a good medium for the growth of microorganisms. This creates a lot of problems not only to prevent milk from curding/souring but also to protect from pathogens causing a variety of diseases in human system.

Diseases Spread through Unclean Milk

Through Cows

1. Tuberculosis
2. Milk sickness
3. Undulant fever
4. Pox
5. Anthrax

Through Milkers

1. Typhoid
2. Paratyphoid
3. Dysentery

4. Diarrhoea
5. Diptheria
6. Scarlet fever
7. Cholera
8. Spetic sore throat
9. Gastro-enteritis

Note: (1) These milk borne diseases can be prevented from spreading in human being by production of clean and safe milk.

Mastitis and Eradicagtion Programme

Mastitis is a disease of udder in which inflammation of mammary glands is caused by either bacteria, virus or fungi pathogens. Usually the pathogenic bacterial caused organisms are *Staphytococci* and *Corymbacterium*. Predisposing factors of its infection are in sanitary wet floor conditions, injury to the teats, faulty use of milking machine, poor milking hygiene and high yielding animals.

References

Brody, J.E. 2003. Hindustan times Wednesday 7th Jan. 2003.

Gupta, M., Podda G.S. and Bazwa, V. 2003. *Indian farmers' Digest*. 36, 3, 20-27.

Kansal, V.K. 2004. *Indian Dairyman* 56, 5, 46.

Makhel, S., Prabha, S., Mandal, S. and Kanawgia, S.K. *Indian Dairyman*. 56, 2, 49-59.

Prasad, J. 2001. AH and Dairy Science, pp. 551, Kalyani Publishers, Ludhiana.

Sabikhi, L. and Mathur, R.N. 2001. *Indian J. Dairy Sci*. 54, 4, 178-185.

Chapter 14

Prospects of Milk and Indigenous Dairy Products and Dairy Development in North Eastern Region

S.S. Khare

Pro-Vice-Chancellor, North Eastern Hill University, Tura Campus, Tura

The cattle raising in India is as ancient as Aryan Civilization. Traditionally cattle have been raised by people (i) for prestige (ii) as a subsidiary occupation to crop production in rural areas (iv) for meat, fuel, cow dung and bullocks etc. To a great extent this is still the state of affairs. However, through systemic planning by the Government in the form of various Dairy Development programmes starting from Key Village Scheme (during the first three Five Year Plans), the Intensive Cattle Development Project introduced in sixties, Operation Flood I in 1970, Operation Flood II in 1982 and Operation Flood III in 1994, India has reached the present estimated milk production level of more than 90 million tones/year topping the world in terms of milk production as against production of only 17 million tones in 1950. We should be proud of this. India at present contributes 11 per cent of the total world milk production. The estimated cattle population in India in 2004 is more than 200 millions which is 15 per cent of the total cattle population in the whole world and India's buffalo population is 54 per cent of the world's buffalo population.

Even though, India has made phenomenal progress in the area of dairy development, the achievement seems to be insignificant when viewed against the challenges faced by the dairy sector. Although we have huge cattle and buffalo population in the country, but due to huge human population of the country, the per capita availability of milk every day at present is about 230 gm which is quite low, although it is much higher than 125 gm in 1950. It is to be noted that New Zealand tops this list with 8.5 kg/day as per capita availability. Further, very low productivity of milch animals, huge expenditure involved in planning and implementing dairy development projects and under utilization of the large installed capacities of dairy plants are some of the challenges faced by the country in terms of its dairy development.

Because of socio-economical reasons, there are huge number of small and scattered herds in the country which is a big bottleneck for proper economic viability of dairy development. The investment in dairying has decreased from.82 per cent of the total plan expenditure in the First Plan to.52 per cent in the 9th Five Year Plan. This has caused serious constraints for manpower development, creation of proper communication, infrastructure, reliable data base and strengthening of extension network in rural areas. Lack of flow of latest technologies and know how from labs to the cattle farmers and development of suitable technology to suit different rural areas and its socio-economic condition have been bottleneck in dairy development. The major constraints observed in cross breeding has been low reproductivity through artificial insemination, high incidence of repeat breeding in cross breeds, indiscriminate breeding and slaughtering of high yielding animals, ill equipped artificial insemination centres and inadequate expert services. Approximately 80 per cent of the cattle are non-descript local ones which give hardly 1-2 kg/day. Because of this the average milk production per cow in India is approximately 3 kg/day as against about 25 kg/day for average cow in U.S.A. This shows that the milk production can be increased many-folds by having more and more high breed animals in place of non-descript local animals in phases.

In addition to high genetic cattle, balanced feeding of dairy animals is the basis for successful dairy farming. Poor availability of quality feeds and fodder results in low production of milk, shortage of supply of essential nutrients resulting in poor growth and reproduction. Lack of knowledge on the part of farmers about balanced feed, quality feeds and fodder, and lack of organized markets for quality feeds and fodder add to the dimension of the problem. Another problem in speedy dairy development is lack of facilities and lack of knowledge on the part of dairy farmers about disease prevention and control of cattle.

Table 14.1: Annual Milk Production in Different States of NE Region (000' tones)

Sl.No.	*States*	*1981-82*	*1991-92*
1.	Assam	469.00	639.0
2.	Manipur	62.00	83.0
3.	Meghalaya	58.00	50.0
4.	Nagaland	3.45	44.0
5.	Sikkim	18.00	29.0
6.	Tripura	17.50	32.0

Table 14.2: Estimates of Milk Production in NE Region 1997-98 (000 MT)

Sl.No.	*States*	*MilkProduction*
1.	Arunachal Pradesh	44.0
2.	Assam	775.0
3.	Manipur	62.0
4.	Meghalaya	59.0
5.	Mizoram	20.0
6.	Nagaland	46.0
7.	Sikkim	35.0
8.	Tripura	47.0

At present not more than 20 per cent of milk is being processed in the dairy plants under government, organized private and co-operative sectors. The absence of regular and remunerative market for milk and milk products is a major constraints encountered by farmers specially from rural areas. Lack of inadequate credit facilities to the dairy farmers and exploitation by middlemen hampers the farmers from deriving proper profit from dairying and sometimes causes discouragement and frustration to the farmers.

Table 14.3: Projected Milk Production upto Year 1998-99 to 2005-06 (000' tones)

Sl.No.	States	1998-99	2002-03	2004-05	2005-06
1.	Assam	815.32	940.58	1010.25	1047.00
2.	Manipur	99.73	112.72	119.84	123.56
3.	Meghalaya	54.88	56.88	57.91	58.44
4.	Nagaland	105.85	190.04	254.64	294.75
5.	Sikkim	40.49	49.45	54.65	57.45
6.	Tripura	47.21	58.75	65.54	69.23

Table 14.4: Share of Cow, Buffalo and Goat Milk to Total Milk Production in NE States (000' MT) – 1993-94

Sl.No.	States	Cow	Buffalo	Goat	Total
1.	Arunachal Pradesh	21.0	-	-	21.0
2.	Assam	561.0	91.0	24.0	676.0
3.	Manipur	63.0	21.0	-	84.0
4.	Meghalaya	50.0	3.0	-	53.0
5.	Mizoram	9.0	-	-	9.0
6.	Nagaland	42.0	2.0	1.0	45.0
7.	Sikkim	NA	NA	NA	30.0
8.	Tripura	NA	NA	NA	35.0

Dairy extension activities are always treated as secondary due to which most of the dairy farmers are not aware of various aspects of economically profitable dairy farming and the facilities available to them by various organizations. Inadequate communication, transportation and veterinary services located at far distances also contribute to the dairy development adversely.

It calls for a thorough discussion on the part of dairy scientists, policy markers, extension personnel and dairy farmers to address these constraints which may vary from place to place in degree. Use of Participatory Rural Appraisal, more intensive extension activities for effective flow of technologies and informations from lab and other relevant organizations to dairy farmers may help not only in identifying the problems faced by dairy farmers but also in finding possible suitable solutions.

Table 14.5: Per Capita Availability of Milk 1997-98 in NE States (gms/day)

Sl.No.	States	1993-94	1997-98
1.	Arunachal Pradesh	62.0	118.0
2.	Assam	78.0	82.0
3.	Manipur	118.0	79.0
4.	Meghalaya	77.0	78.0
5.	Mizoram	32.0	64.0
6.	Nagaland	93.0	84.0
7.	Sikkim	186.0	191.0
8.	Tripura	33.0	40.0

The scenario of dairy development in North Eastern Region is all the more discouraging. Historically Shillong being the only important city in N.E Region, Britishers for their own consumption wanted to have high breed cattle in Shillong. They brought one bull of Holstein-Friesian breed from Orissa and another bull of Brown Swiss breed from Germany and arranged to start a multiple cross breed cattle farm in Shillong with the help of Nepalese. They encouraged Nepalese to rear cattle. The oldest cattle farm in N.E. Region was the one established in 1924 in Upper Shillong. At one time there were about 1000 cattle of mixed breeds (Holstein-Friesian, Jersey, Brown Swiss). Another cattle farm was established in Khanapara, Assam in 1926. Artificial insemination was started in Shillong in around 1965. In 1987 during Operation Flood-II, National Dairy Development Board offered the states of N.E. Region for production of wholesome milk and its distribution at a reasonable price by collecting milk from the producers door-steps regularly paying its remuneration through Amul pattern cooperative system. Only Assam Government accepted the offer in 1987 with the establishment of West Assam Milk Producers Cooperative Union Limited (WAMCUL) in 1987. Nagaland followed 5 years later by establishing Kohima Milk Union Limited (KOMUL) in 1992. Assam has taken up an Agricultural Infrastructural Development Project through World Bank in 1998, which is likely to boost dairy development.

The number of high breed cattle of high yield variety rose to 25 lakh in 1965 in N.E. Region which was approximately 30 per cent of the total cattle. A large number of Nepalese and Biharis were involved in this sector. But due to Nepalese and Biharis Hatao drive by local people of this region, this number has come down to only 18 lakhs at present which is only 15 per cent of the total cattle in NE Region. This has happened in a big way in Meghalaya. Because of this, the total annual milk production in Meghalaya which steadily rose from 39,000 tones in 1970 to 64,000 tonnes in 1984, dropped down to only 46,000 tones in 1985 and could rise to only 62,000 tonnes in 2001.

Table 14.6: Project per Capita Availability of Milk in NE States in 2004-05 and 2005-06 (gms)

Sl.No.	*States*	*2004-05 (gms)*	*2005-06 (gms)*
1.	Assam	93.53	94.88
2.	Manipur	135.37	136.62
3.	Meghalaya	67.72	66.88
4.	Nagaland	436.87	495.01
5.	Sikkim	279.01	287.01
6.	Tripura	49.33	51.00

Note: Requirement of milk has been worked out on the basis of recommended norms of 220 gms per day per capita by the ICMR.

The largest cooling plant was established in Naya Banglow (near Shillong) in 1962 which is dry due to Nepalese and Biharis Hatao drive in Meghalaya. Subsequently the government established another chilling plant along with pasteurizing unit in 1983 in Shillong which is still functioning. One pasteurization plant was established in Khanapara in 1962 to cater the needs of dairy farmers around Guwahati.

Amongst 8 states of N.E. Region, Assam is well ahead in terms of milk production (850/1300 thousands tones), milk processing Units (9/13), liquid milk plants (9/22), organized dairy cooperative (123/404) and the number of cattle 12000/16000 thousands). After

Assam, Sikkim has done significantly well in terms of per capita availability of milk which is around 200 gm as against 80 gm being the average per capita availability of milk in N.E. region and 125 gm being per capita availability of milk in Assam as in 2000. Sikkim also has (162/402) organized Dairy Cooperative Societies and is top in the list of states in N.E. Region. Nagaland has been doing extremely well during the 4-5 years and the projected per capita availability of milk in 2004-05 is 436 gm/day for Nagaland as against 280 gm/day that of Sikkim and 90 gm/day that of N.E. Region average and 230 gm/day that of National average. Mizoram's performance is significant in terms of average milk yield/cross breed cattle which is 8.5 kg as against 8.4 that of Meghalaya, 8.00 that of Manipur and 4.5 being average of NE Region for cross breed cattle.

Table 14.7: Average Milk Yield of Cows, Buffaloes and Goats in NE States in 1991 (in litre/day)

Sl.No.	*States*	*Cow*		*Buffalo*	*Goat*
		Non-descript	*Cross-breed*		
1.	Arunachal Pradesh	1.030	4.56	NA	NA
2.	Assam	0.912	3.74	1.770	0.227
3.	Manipur	1.400	7.96	3.16	NA
4.	Meghalaya	0.720	8.410	1.96	NA
5.	Mizoram	0.710	8.500	NA	NA
6.	Nagaland	1.710	6.760	3.160	0.380

Looking at the very low per capita availability of milk in NE Region which is around 90 gm/day as against minimum requirement of 250 gm/day for a person as per Indian Council of Medical Research, there is a tremendous scope of dairy development in this region. It will not be out of way to mention here that the annual consumption of Amul Taja (milk) in N.E. Region is more than worth Rs 28 crores and that of other milk products from Amul is about Rs.12 crores. Further, annual consumption of milk products at sufficient high cost say Rs 25/ltt from other companies of West Bengal is also of the order of Rs.12 crores. Because of lack of availability of fresh milk and its products, people here are compelled to go for Amul and other Company's milk and milk products. If we can increase milk production to fulfill the demand of people here, they will prefer to buy pure fresh milk and its product at a rate about 70 per cent of the rates of Amul Taja and its products which are 3-4 months old. In N.E. Region, Khoa and chhenna based milk products are very common. In addition to this Paneer and Sweet Dahi is also quite popular. Some of the main bottlenecks in dairy development in this region are (i) lack of awareness and information about dairy prospects (ii) lack of high quality breeds (iii) non-availability of quality feed and fodder (iv) lack of marketing net work (v) lack of transportation and communication (vi) geographical constraints (vii) lack of veterinary hospitals, breeding farms, artificial insemination facilities (viii) lack of awareness about the nutritional and medicinal value of milk and its products.

Table 14.8: Total Number of Cattle, Buffalo and Goat in NE States in 1992 (in 000)

Sl.No.	States	Cattle	Buffalo	Goat
1.	Arunachal Pradesh	324.0	5	125
2.	Assam	10118.0	959	3454
3.	Manipur	719	114	38
4.	Meghalaya	535	33	195
5.	Mizoram	59	7	21
6.	Nagaland	332	32	151
7.	Sikkim	198	2	114
8.	Tripura	949	20	429

Looking at the acute unemployment, this is high time that youth should be encouraged to take up dairy farming/processing/ management as self employment opportunity. Agriculture Universities, Indian Institute of Entrepreneurship, NIRD, S I R D and other related Institutions should give short term training programme in different aspects of dairy development. The funding agencies should also come forward in this direction. Dairy farmers should be given required know how and should be encouraged to produce high quality feeds and fodder. ICAR, KVK, KGK etc. may play an active role in this direction. Awareness camp may be organized from time to time at block level to create awareness about the nutritional and medicinal value of milk and its products and about dairy prospects in this region. NGO's, academic institutions,

ICAR can contribute significantly towards this. Government should establish high pedigree breeding farms, A.I. centres, and animal health care units at block level and the dairy farmers should be encouraged to rare high breed cattle instead of non-descript cattle. They should also be given required know how about maintenance and management of high breed cattle. Government should open milk chilling centres, small unit dairy plants at block level.

Table 14.9: Annual Growth Rate of Milking Cows and Buffaloes in NE States–1992

Sl.No.	*States*	*Annual Growth Rate of Milking Cows (per cent)*	*Annual Growth Rate of Milking Buffaloes (per cent)*
1.	Arunachal Pradesh	(-) 3.58	(-) 12.94
2.	Assam	6.75	1.031
3.	Manipur	4.56	0.00
4.	Meghalaya	0.00	0.00
5.	Mizoram	8.45	0.00
6.	Nagaland	8.76	14.87
7.	Sikkim	1.61	0.00
8.	Tripura	11.46	3.13

Table 14.10: Milk Production Status in NE States in 1998-99

Sl.No.	*States*	*Milk Production (000'MT)*
1.	Assam	44.5
2.	Assam	798.0
3.	Manipur	65.0
4.	Meghalaya	61.0
5.	Mizoram	21.5
6.	Nagaland	47.5
7.	Sikkim	40.0
8.	Tripura	45.0

I am sure that if the above mentioned measures are taken at block level, then within 5 years we can increase the production of milk and its products to at least double of what it is today in N.E.

Region. We have made a humble beginning in this direction by training students of Rural Development and Agricultural Production in dairy farming, by developing a model dairy farm in the campus and by encouraging students to take up dairy as an opportunity for self employment. We have also conducted some orientation programmes to create awareness in this region. We have also conducted some participating Rural Appraisal programs on neighboring villages. But this is too little. A lot lot more is to he done.

Table 14.11: No. of Milk Processing Factories and No. of Liquid Milk Plants as on 31.3.1997 in NE States

Sl.No.	*States*	*No. of Milk ProcessingFactories*	*No. of Liquid Milk Plant*
1.	Arunachal Pradesh	Not reported	1
2.	Assam	9	9
3.	Manipur	-	1
4.	Meghalaya	-	6
5.	Mizoram	-	1
6.	Nagaland	1	1
7.	Sikkim	2	2
8.	Tripura	1	1

Table 14.12: State Dairy Cooperatives in NE States as on 31.3.1998

Sl.No.	*States*	*Dairy Coop. Societies, Organized (No)*	*Farmer Members ('000)*	*Rural Milk Procurement (000 kg/ day)*	*Milk Marketing (000 l/day)*	*Processing Capacities (000 L/day)*
1.	Assam	123	2	3	6	60
2.	Nagaland	35	1	1	1	-
3.	Sikkim	162	5	7	7	15
4.	Tripura	84	4	1	5	10

There have been operation fold program in three phases in the country so far. But their important in north eastern region has not been significant. I think north-eastern region needs a special programme Operation Flood north-east. To boost dairy activities in north-east region I take this opportunities to appeal dairy scientist, policy makers, Indian dairy board, ICAR, KVK, KVG, NIRD, SIRD, Agricultural Universities and other concerned organization. In north-eastern region to jointly convey forward to meet the objective. This will not only boost dairy development but also give self-employment opportunities to thousand of unemployed youth of northeastern region.

Table 14.13: No. of Dairy Plants Registered Under MMPO as on June 1, 1996 in NE States (capacity 000 lit/day)

States	*Cooperative*	*Private*	*Others*	*Total*
Mizoram	1	-	-	1
Tripura	1	-	-	1
Sikkim	13	-	-	13

Table 14.14: Capacity of MMPO Registration by Central Registering Authority as on March 1991

States	*District*	*Name*
Sikkim	East Sikkim	Sikkim Co-op. Milk Producers Union Ltd.
Tripura	East Tripura	The Tripura Dist. Milk Producers Union Ltd.

With these words, I would like to thanks once again Professor Pandey and its team of organizing committees for inviting me to share my opinion and thoughts regarding the prospects of milk and milk products in north-east region.

Dairy Cooperatives in North East States

Assam

1. Cachar and Karimganj Dist. Milk Producers Cooperative Union Ltd., Silchar.
2. DSD Cooperative Milk Producers Union Ltd., Jorhat.
3. West Assam Milk Producers Cooperative Union Ltd., Khanapara, Panjabari, Guwahati-781002.

Mizoram

1. Mizoram Coop. Milk Producers Union Ltd., C/O Directorate of Animal Husbandry and Veterinary, Govt. of Mizoram, Aizawl-796001.

2. Mizoram Multi-commodity Producers Cooperative Union Ltd., Aizawl, Mizoram-796017. Brand Name : MULCO Milk.

Nagaland

1. Bhola MPCS Ltd., Dimapur-797112 (Dairy Products and sale of milk).
2. Chumukedima III MPCS, Dimapur. (Buy and sale of milk).
3. Dairy Farms MPCS, Dimapur. (Sale of milk)
4. Everst MPCS, Dimapur (Buy and sale of milk)
5. Kohima Milk Union Ltd., Dimapur (Sale of milk)
6. Medziphema MPCS, Medziphema (Milk products and sale of milk)
7. NC MPCS, Kedima, Dimapur (Milk sale).
8. Tulovi Milk Producers Cooperative Society, Dimapur (Buy and sale of milk)
9. Valley Milk Producers Cooperative Society, Dimapur (Buy and sale of milk).

Sikkim

Sikkim Cooperative Milk Producers Union Ltd., Gangtok 737102 (Milk processing).

Tripura

Tripura Cooperative Milk Producers Union Ltd., Agartala-799006 (Dairy Product preparation -Brand name – GOMATI)

Dairy Products Manufacture and Suppliers in NE States

Assam

1. Govt. of Assam, Directorate of Dairy Development, Khanapara, Guwahati (Products – Milk, Ghee, Paneer etc.)
2. Radhesham Enterprises, Fancy Bazar, Guwahati (Dealers in all dairy products).

State Govt. Listing

Arunachal Pradesh

- ☆ Area: 93,743 sq.km
- ☆ Population: 8,58,392

Livestock Population (Census 1997)

1. Cattle: 4,52,920
2. Buffalo: 17,483
3. Sheep: 28,245
4. Goat: 1,83,826

Assam

- ☆ Area: 78,438 sq.km
- ☆ Population: 2,22,94,562

Livestock Population

1. Cattle: 77,85,717
2. Buffalo: 6,51,819
3. Sheep: 77,404
4. Goat: 26,44,704

Manipur

- ☆ Area: 22,327 sq.km
- ☆ Population: 18,62,714

Livestock Population

1. Cattle: 5,08,262
2. Buffalo: 95,249
3. Sheep: 7,533
4. Goat: 32,942

Meghalaya

- ☆ Area: 22,429 sq.km
- ☆ Population: 17,60,626

Livestock Population

1. Cow: 1,89,000 (Non-descript)
2. Cow: 10,000 (Cross breed)
3. Buffalo: 10,000

- ☆ Total milk production – 59,000 tonnes up to 1997-98

  Milk Plant: 6 Nos.

  Feed unit: 2 Nos.

  Breeding farm: 4 Nos.

Mizoram

- ☆ Area: 21,081 sq.km
- ☆ Population: 6,86,217

Livestock Population

1. Cattle (Male): 12,025
2. Cattle (Female): 40,856
3. Buffalo (Male): 2,102
4. Buffalo (Female): 5,345

Nagaland

- ☆ Area: 16,579 sq.km
- ☆ Population: 12,15,573

Livestock Population

1. Cow: 70,000 (Cross breed)
2. Cow: 9,000 (Non-descript)
3. Buffalo: 9,000

Tripura

- ☆ Area: 10,486 sq.km
- ☆ Population: 27,44,827

Livestock Population

1. Cow: 2,55,000 (Non-descript)
2. Cow: 45,000 (Cross breed)
3. Buffalo: 7,000

References

Mudgal, V.D., Singhal, K.K. and Sharma, D.D. Advances of Dairy Animal Production, International Book Distributing Co., 2003.

Ramasamy, D., Shibu, A.V. and Gopi, H. Dairy Technologist's Hand Book, International Book Distributing Co., 1999.

Venkatasubramanian, V., Singh, A.K., Rao, S.V.N. Dairy Development in India, Concept Publishing Co., New Delhi, 2003.

Winton, A.L. and Winton, K.B. Milk and Milk Products, Agrobios, India, 2000.

Meghalaya Socio-Economic Review : Government of Meghalaya, Directorate of Economics and Statistics, Shillong, 2003.

Where do we Stand in 2003 Meghalaya and North East and India and the World: Govt. of Meghalaya, Directorate of Economics and Statistics, Meghalaya, Shillong, 2004.

Meghalaya Achievements in 30 years 1972-73 to 2001-2002; Govt. of Meghalaya, Directorate of Economics and Statistics, Shillong, 2002.

Pocket Statistical Hand Book Meghalaya, Directorate of Economics and Statistics, Govt. of Meghalaya, Shillong, 2003.

Statistical Hand Book of Manipur, Directorate of Economics and Statistics, Govt. of Manipur, Imphal, 2002.

Mizoram Statistical Hand Book 2000, Directorate of Economics and Statistics, Govt. of Mizoram, 2001.

Statistical Hand Book of Nagaland, 2000, Directorate of Economics and Statistics, Govt. of Nagaland, Kohima, 2001.

All India Dairy Business Directory (Dairy Year Book), 2001, Special Millennium Issue, Sadana Publishers and Distributors, Second Edition.

Chapter 15

Paneer: An Important Indigenous Milk Product in Indian Perspectives

A.B. Mojumdar
Plant Animal Relationship Division,
Indian Grassland and Fodder Research Institute,
Jhansi – 284 003, U.P.

India ranks first amongst the milk producing countries globally contributing 16 per cent of the total milk in the world. The total milk production is around 87 million tones which has paved the Indian industry emerging as the sunrise industry. Indigenous milk products in our country have found place in the rapidly growing markets in the international area. NDDB (Amul), Varuna, Nandini, Sanchi, Verka etc. are few of notable examples who are emerging as leaders in the manufacture of indigenous dairy products.

Paneer: An Important Indigenous Dairy Product

There are wide range of indigenous milk products like Dahi (Yoghurt), butter, ghee, paneer, cheese, khoa and wide range of secondary products prepared out of them which find place in Indian dishes. As a matter of fact, rural part of our country may be considered more suited to dairy industry. The product market comprising of cheese, paneer and milk powder has grown from 83.7 thousand tones in 1997 to 86.7 thousand tones in 2000 (Dairy India, 2001). As a result of and phosphorion, the consumption of milk products has tremendously increased especially amongst the younger generations.

Paneer is one of the important indigenous dairy product and has gained its significance in recent time as it is nutritionally balanced, possess mild flavour, economic, simple to manufacture commercially and suits the Indian food habits. It is believed that approximately 5 per cent of total milk produced in India is converted to Paneer (Mathur, 1991). It is following a boom in the consumption as well as its production (Rao *et al.*, 1992). It is nevertheless, an important indigenous milk product which is used as base material for the preparation of large number of culinary dishes, sandwiches, snacks and sweet (Kanaujia and Rizvi, 2003). Paneer making practice was earlier chiefly confined to northern and eastern region of our country but now has started growing popularity in other parts of country.

Historical Background of Paneer

Paneer as acid- coagulated indigenous milk product was first introduced in India by Persian and Afgan invaders who curdled the surplus milk with the help of sour milk pieces or creeper called "Punika" bark of Palasa tree (Indian Dairyman, 1989). Emergence of solid white mass from mixture of warm milk and curd during Kusna and Saka Satavanam periods appears to be the earlies allusion of heat- acid coagulated milk product. During last three decades, Indian dairy industry has undergone revolutionary changes in its structure. Several units have now also been commissioned for the preparation of paneer.

Physical Attributes of Paneer

Typically paneer is white in appearance with spongy body, close-knit texture possessing sweetish acidic nutty flavour (Verma and Mathur, 1987). Paneer contains almost all fat and casein alongwith part of whey protein, minerals and vitamins present in the milk. It is relatively low in sugar content, highly nutritions and wholesome.

Milk Quality and its Relevance to Paneer Quality

Quality of milk used for paneer making has direct relevance on the quality of paneer. Besides, quality of paneer varies from one manufacturer to another which depends upon several factors like type of milk source (cow/buffalo/goat), fat content, type of coagulant, heat treatment etc. However, quality of milk used for paneer making has limited control in rural areas and unorganized sector. As compared to rural areas, however, paneer is chiefly made in urban sector.

The titrable acidity of acidic milk ranges between 0.20-0.23 per cent. Excess of acidity from this limit, may lead to inferior quality of product. The paneer such formed becomes unpalatable when acidity of milk is more than 0.28 per cent (Dairy, 1980). Low fat level (3.5 per cent) of milk tends to make paneer soft and spongy (Chawla *et al.*, 1985). Increase in the fat content of raw milk results in increase in the fat content of paneer and decline in the protein and carbohydrate content of paneer. The moisture content in the paneer exhibit inverse relationship with the fat content of milk (Sachdeva and Singh, 1988). Ghodekar (1989) recommended 5 per cent fat level in the raw milk suitable for paneer making. Buffalo milk containing 6 per cent fat and 9 per cent SNF has been found to make high quality paneer (Kumar and Bictor, 1991, Syed *et al.*, 1992).

Choice of Animal Species Suited for Paneer Making

For the preparation of good quality paneer, buffalo milk is considered more suitable than cow milk as the later one yields an inferior product in terms of body and texture as well as desirable frying properties (Sachdeva *et al.*, 1985, Singh and Kanaujia, 1988). The lack of large size fat globules in cow milk is probably on reason for the poor quality of its product in form of paneer as relatively larger size of fat globules facilitates in spongy behaviour of paneer.

Generally, the paneer prepared from buffalo milk is hard and rubbery in nature as it is found to contain higher level of casein and minerals. Paneer prepared from buffalo milk can easily tolerate rigorous cooking (Ghodekar, 1989). Paneer made from buffalo milk is also rich in protein, fat, ash and dry matter content. Boghra and Mathur (1995) compared paneer prepared from buffalo and cow milk and observed that paneer out of buffalo 25.65 Vs 23.0 per cent fat, 1.98 Vs 1.46 per cent ash content and 49.1 Vs 45.3 per cent dry matter than cow milk's paneer. However, soluble mineral as a percent of total mineral has been found lower in buffalo milk paneer than cow. Lipid profile namely total lipid, and phosphor lipid and cholesterol contents is similar in both cow and buffalo milk paneer (Pal *et al.*, 1996). Calcium content is higher (54.25 mg/100 gm) in buffalo milk paneer than cow milk paneer (52.0 mg/100 g) whereas sodium and potassium content are higher in cow milk (Boghra *et al.*, 1998) paneer. Cow milk reconstituted with buffalo milk is also recommended so that fat and SNF ratio should maintained 1:2 (Tewari and Sachdeva, 1991). Cow milk in combination with soyabean is also reported to yield good quality paneer with soft and hollow texture. Paneer can also be prepared from goat milk. Paneer prepared from Jamunapari and Barbari goat has been found to contain 5.98 and 4.99 per cent fat, 14.90 and 14.19 per cent TS, 8.92 and 9.19 per cent SNF, 3.29 and 3.36 per cent casein. Paneer yield is

Table 15.1: Defect Observed in Paneer and Measures for their Prevention

Sl.No.	*Defect*	*Preventive Measures*
		Appearance
(1)	Dry surface	Optimize (lower) fat content of milk
(2)	Surface hardening	Avoid surface drying during manufacture. Package in better moisture-barrier packaging material
(3)	Unclean	Insist on sanitary practices and use good quality milk
(4)	Brown colouration/ spots	Avoid overheated surfaces of equipment.
		Body & Texture
(1)	Coarse texture	Use fresh milk
		Standardize fat: SNF ration to be 1:1.65 Standardize coagulation temperature (70ºC and pH 5.3)
		Optimize fat in milk (5.8%)
(2)	Hard body	Standardize coagulation, heating and cooling condition during manufacture
		Flavour
(1)	Sour	Use fresh milk and normal titratable acidity.
		Follow recommended coagulating acid, concentration, temperature and volume
(2)	Oxidized/rancid	Store paneer at 4°C to avoid hydrolysis/ oxidation of milk fat
(3)	State/Foreign	Reduce storage period at 4°C to control microbial growth
(4)	Smoky/burnt	Avoid overheated milk and smoky atmosphere

higher in Jamunapari goat milk than Barbari goat (Pal and Agnihotri, 1996). However, it lacks compact mass and therefore less acceptable.

Table 15.2: Nutrient Composition (Per cent) of Paneer

Sample Source	*Constituent*					*References*
	Moisture	*Total Solids*	*Fat*	*Protein*	*Ash*	
Buffalo milk (5 per cent fat)	56.77	43.22	22.30	-	-	Bhattacharya *et al.* (1971)
Buffalo milk (5.5 per cent fat)	55.19	44.81	23.80	17.99	-	Chawla *et al.* (1987)
Buffalo milk (6 per cent fat)	48.30	51.70	29.20	18.50	-	Desai (1988)
Cow milk (4 per cent fat)	52.40	47.60	23.40	20.30	-	-do-
Mixed milk (5 per cent fat)	49.00	51.00	26.10	20.80	-	-do-
Buffalo milk (5.9 per cent)	51.12	48.88	26.86	17.38	2.00	Dharmapal and Garg (1989)
Buffalo milk (5.8 per cent fat)	50.72	49.28	27.13	17.99	1.87	Rajorhia *et al.* (1984)
Market sample	51.91	48.09	26.59	17.65	1.78	-do-
Buffalo milk (5.8 per cent fat)	54.10	45.90	23.50	18.20	1.80	Sachdeva and Singh (1987)
Buffalo milk (5 per cent fat)	56.43	43.57	22.50	-	-	Shukla *et al.* (1984)
Mixed milk (5 per cent fat)	57.14	42.86	22.32	-	-	-do-
Cow milk (5 per cent fat)	53.90	46.10	24.80	17.60	-	Singh and Kanaujia (1988)

Chapter 16

Effluent Treatment and Disposal in Dairy Industry: A Case Study

P.N. Reddy
Head (QI and PD)
Mother Dairy, Delhi – 110092

Waste Generation and Disposal

The latest Management slogan is Zero Waste. This may be possible in some Industries but in a Dairy Industry this is still a distant reality. Because in the production, processing and manufacture of milk products a certain amount of waste is imminent. Such a waste may be due to the useless portions of the raw materials required in the manufacture or unavoidable losses in the process involved in the manufacture. If the waste is a solid its disposal can be done either by burying or landfilling. However, if it is a liquid waste the easy way is to drain it into a river or lake.

Environmental Management System which is popularly known as ISO-14001 is being followed by many Industries around the World. It is a system which regulates all resources utilized in the Industry. Pollution Prevention is taken care under this system. Many activities were started and being continued for water conservation which has resulted in less use of water. Rain water harvesting has resulted in increase in water table.

At Mother Dairy the treated wastewater is utilized for gardening purpose and the dried sludge as manure. The canteen waste is converted into Wormi/Vermi Compost.

Mother Dairy is certified not only for ISO:9002, HACCP but also for ISO-14001.

Regulations about Waste Discharge

Over the years the discharge of wastes have increased and regulations were imposed in various countries all over the world making it mandatory on the part of the industries to treat the waste before it is discharged into the rivers or lakes to avoid pollution of water. India is no exception in this regard and an Act was passed in the 1974 to prevent and control water pollution followed by Air, Environment (Protection), Hazards Waste Handling Acts and Rules.

Dairy Waste Generation in India

Regarding dairy industry in India, improved facilities to farmers and wider use of mechanical refrigeration have made it possible to collect milk over considerable areas and to bring it to a large central processing plant either for marketing as fluid milk or conversion into products. This has resulted in greater concentration of waste and the dairy waste being rich in nutrients may endanger aquatic life it let into rivers or lakes without treatment. A dissolved oxygen level of 7 PPM is present in rivers or lakes and if this level reaches below 5 PPM the aquatic life is in danger because the micro-organisms present in the waste or in the water of the river or lake use the dissolved oxygen to convert the organic matter constituting of protein, lactose etc. into end products. Hence it has become necessary for the dairy industry to treat its waste before it is discharged into rivers or lakes.

This paper does not deal with the engineering aspect of the treatment plant but only the process involved in the treatment of dairy waste water with specific reference to Delhi Mother Dairy Effluent Treatment Plant. Activated sludge process, a biological treatment to the waste is being used for treating the waste at Delhi Mother Dairy.

Activated Sludge: Treatment Process Concept

The raw effluent, comprising of dairy waste, and domestic waste bears oil and grease, high amount of suspended solids and biochemical oxygen demand. The conceptual approach of the treatment includes the removal of oil and grease, coarses and settleable suspended particles, dissolved organic matters and handling of sludge for disposal. Substantial amount of free oil and grease is removed by skimming operation in the grease trap. However, the heart of this treatment system in the aerobic biological reactors which are designed on the basis of activated sludge process. The activated sludge treatment process basically involves the degradation of organic matter by the action of various microorganisms as depicted in the following equation.

$$\text{Organics} + \text{Micro-organisms} + \text{Oxygen} + \text{Nutrients} + \text{New cells} \rightarrow \text{Carbon-dioxide} + \text{Ammonia} + \text{Energy}$$

This could be restated as:

$$\text{Waste} + \text{Sludge} + \text{Air} - \text{Surplus Sludge} + \text{End products}$$

In this biological process, a part of the newly synthesized sludge undergoes oxidation called endogenous respiration.

$$\text{Cells} + \text{Oxygen} - \text{End Products} + \text{less cells}$$

The efficiency of the system mainly depends upon the concentration of active microorganisms present to perform the assimilation of organic matter. The activated sludge, in general, consists bacterial and microorganisms like protozoa, rotifiers, etc. The desirably environmental conditions like sufficient dissolved oxygen, substrate and nutrients are required for cell growth and energy for various metabolic functions. It is essential that the biological floc should readily separate from the treated wastewater in thè final clarifier. The concentration of microflora is maintained by routing the mixed liquor flowing from the aeration tank through a secondary clarifier and recycling most of the settled biological solids back to the aeration tank.

Excess or deficient quantity of food (incoming BOD) adversely affects the physical quality of biological sludge. The activated sludge system is designed on the basis of particular food to microorganisms ratio (F/M ratio). For the dairy waste the desired ration is about 0.2. The optimal pH for an active biological aeration system is between 6.5 to 8.5. The surplus biological sludge is discharged into sludge drying beds for dewatering and drying.

Mother Dairy Delhi: A Case Study

Introduction

Delhi Mother Dairy has set up an effluent treatment plant which was commissioned in April 1982. The capacity from 1000 M^3 was increased to 1650 M^3 in 1986. Not only is the waste water treated by the activated sludge process in this plant, but also the sewage from the Dairy and adjoining staff quarters.

Delhi Mother Dairy handles about 8.5 lakh litres of clarified, homogenized and pasteurized toned milk every day and the milk is sent to the retail outlets in the city through insulated road tankers. Depending on the season, major differences occur in the quantities of milk received from cooperative milk federations and in the use of conserved dairy products. Besides milk about 25000 litres of Ice Cream per day is manufactured at Mother Dairy.

Sources of Wastewater Generation

Waste water is generated mainly from:

- ☆ Various CIP Systems
- ☆ Cleaning of floors, equipment, etc.
- ☆ And domestic was from the Milk Plant, Ice Cream Plant and Staff Quarters.

Designed characteristics of the Plant are as under:

Raw Effluent

- ☆ BOD-5 at 20°C: 1200 mg/litre
- ☆ COD: 2500 mg/litre
- ☆ Oil and Grease: 150 mg/litre
- ☆ S.S.: 1000 mg/litre
- ☆ pH: 7.0 – 8.0 sometimes alkaline
- ☆ Temperature: Less than 40°C

Mother Dairy was granted consent to discharge the treated effluent by the Delhi Pollution Control Committee with the following standards:

Parameters	*Prescribed Limit*
Temperature	Not exceeding 5°C than Ambient Temperature
pH	5.5 to 9.0
Total suspended solids	100 mg/litre
BOD-5 at 20°C	30 mg/litre
Oil and Grease	10 mg/litre
COD	250 mg/litre
Detergents	10 mg/litre

Initial Layout of the Plant (Figure 16.1)

The effluent from the Dairy by gravity used to enter the wet well passing through the API Separator which was then pumped into the equalization tanks alongwith the domestic waste generated from the residential complex. Air was bubbled in the equalization tanks with the aid of compressors. From the equalization tanks wastewater was pumped to a primary clariflocculator. There was an arrangement to add alum and lime before the wastewater entered in the flocculation chamber. From the clariflocculator the settled effluent flowed under gravity to aeration tanks. The mixed liquor from the aeration tanks settled in a secondary sedimentation tank. The settled sludge was pumped into the aeration tanks. Periodically it was discharged into the sludge drying beds. The treated effluent was pumped through a long pipeline to Shahdara Outfall Canal which ultimately joined Yamuna river.

Present Layout of the Plant (Figure 16.2)

The treatment system remained mostly same as earlier. Few changes were made.

The API Separator did not work may be due to the less amount of Fat present in the waste or it was acting as a primary settling tank creating frequent chokage of the grease trap. Arrangements was made to by-pass the system even before the expansion which is being followed even now.

The clariflocculator was converted into thickner and the effluent is directly pumped into the aeration tanks.

MOTHER DAIRY EFFLUENT TREATMENT PLANT FLOW DIAGRAM

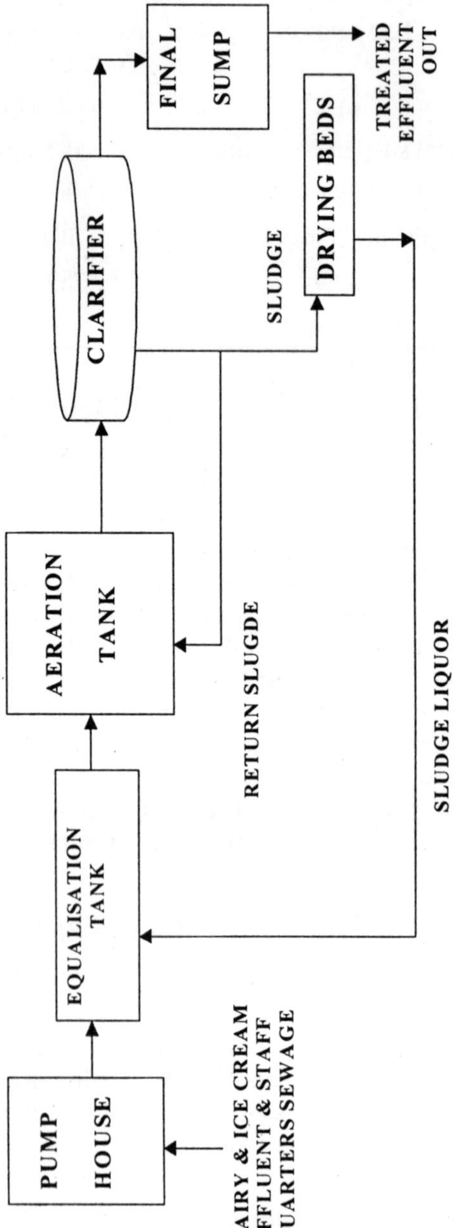

Figure 16.1

SCHEMATIC FLOW DIAGRAM OF MOTHER DAIRY E.T.P

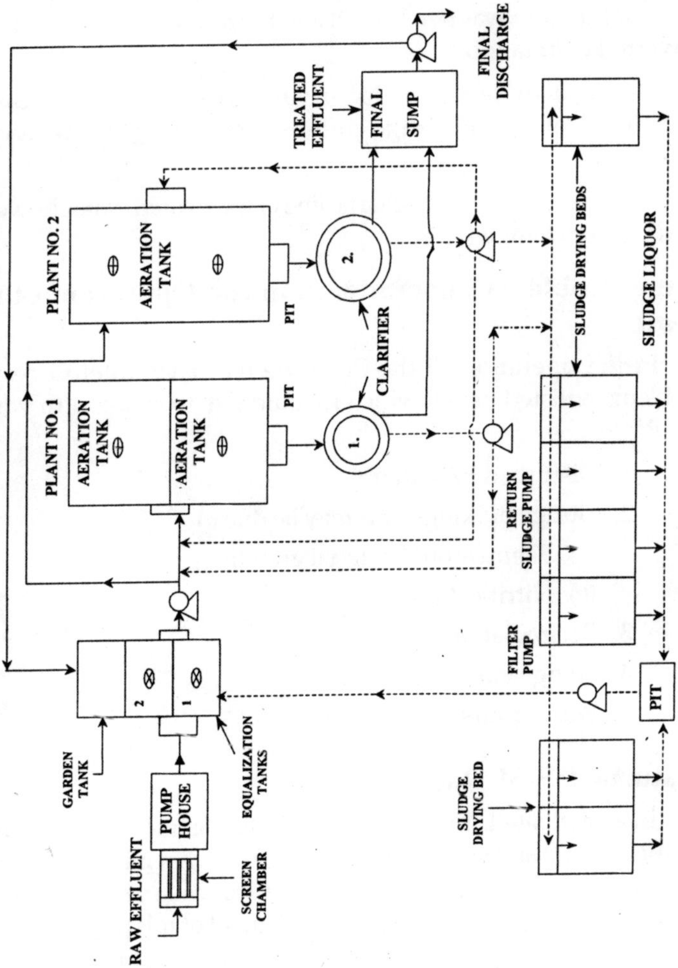

Figure 16.2

An additional aeration tank equal to the initial capacity was provided. Pipelines were provided in such a way that it is possible to run the aeration tanks in series. This facility was given in 1986. In 1987 provisions was also given to run the plant in parallel.

Final clarifier was newly built and the former final clarifier was converted as a standby.

The capacity of the sludge drying beds was also increased. Additional or higher range pumps were provided wherever necessary.

Final sump and the discharge line of the treated water however remained unchanged.

Some Problems Encountered in the Operation of the Plant

In the operation of the Plant we had encountered certain problems enlisted below which I would like to share with you in detail:

1. Disturbed F/M Ratio
2. Sludge bulking : This may be due to
   (*a*) Filamentous bacterial growth;
   (*b*) Nitrification
3. Recirculation of sludge
4. Sludge volumes
5. Foul odours

Disturbed F/M Ratio

In an activated sludge process, waste organics serve as a food for the bacteria and small population of fungi that might be present. The secondary feeders (Protozoa) consumes several thousands bacteria for a single reproduction. The benefit of this predator – prey action is twofold (1) removal of bacteria stimulates further bacterial growth, accelerating metabolism of the organic matter (2) settling characteristics of the biological block is improved by reducing the number of free bacteria in solution. Good settling characteristics occur when an activated sludge is held in the endogenous (starvation) phase. Furthermore, a large population of under-fed organisms remove BOD very rapidly from the solution. Excess microorganisms are wasted from the process to maintain proper balance between food supply and biological mass in the aeration tanks. This balance is referred to as food-to-microorganisms ratio (F/M) which is normally expressed in units of kgs. Of BOD applied per day per kg. of MLSS in the aeration tanks. Operation at high F/M ratio results in incomplete metabolism of the organic matter, poor settling characteristics of the biological floc, and, consequently, poor BOD removal efficiency. At a low F/M ratio, the mass of microorganisms are in a near starvation condition that results in a high degree of organic matter removal, good settleability of activated sludge, and efficient BOD removal.

The plant was designed to have 4000 mg/litre of MLSS with a F/M ration of 0.2. However our experience was that we could not maintain MLSS concentration more than 3000 mg/litre and the F/M ration was between 0.3 to 0.5 which was considered high. Even at this ratio the Plant was running satisfactorily for the last many years.

Sludge Bulking

Filamentous Bacterial Growth

One of the most common problems in aerobic biological treatment is poor settleability of the activated sludge floc. Sometimes this is related to filamentous growths which produce more buoyant flock. As per the literature this is caused by the Bacterium 'Sphaerotilus natans', whose filaments are composed of chains of rod like cells with rounded ends that are encapsulated in a tight polysaccharide sheath. These bacteria grow optimum at 15–40°C at pH 6.5–8.1.

Higher amount of carbohydrates (mono or di-Saccharides) also said to increase the growth of filamentous bacteria. Dairy waste being rich in lactose must be one of the contributing factors for the growth of filamentous bacteria.

Nitrification

The plant was designed with BOD in the influent to be around 1200 mg/litre. Because of the clariflocculator the BOD fed into the aeration tanks was less than 900 mg/litre. This has resulted in over aeration. Generally the DO availability was found more than 2 mg/litre resulting in bulking of the sludge. It is also said that nitrifying bacteria can convert ammonia to nitrate in the aeration tanks and during subsequent detention in the final clarifier the nitrate can be used as an oxygen source under anaerobic conditions, releasing nitrogen gas that buyo up biological floc leading to carryovers in the final clarifier. When the final effluent was very clear for a few days this problem was found to occur.

The best solution to the nitrification problem is to increase sludge waste to deplete the nitrifying bacteria and to decrease the air supply to reduce D.O. levels. In such carryovers we did increase the sludge waste but could not reduce D.O. levels because each chamber of aeration tank contained only one aerator, the speed of which could not be regulated. Stoppage of one aerator lead to anaerobic condition in that particular tank which when taken in line further destabilized the system. This was taken care in the expansion.

Recirculation of Sludge

Recirculation of sludge is of vital importance in maintaining the required MLSS in the system. The excess is taken to the drying beds. Initially, we were advised to have 50 per cent to 60 per cent recirculation of return sludge from the final clarifier back to the aeration tanks. On practice it was observed that desired results were contain only when the recirculation was 85 per cent - 100 per cent.

Sludge Volume

Most of the time the sludge volume remains about 980 ml. Whenever it goes down we observed the final effluent not meeting the laid down standards. This volume was brought to 600 ml by adding "Microlift" a microbial culture in a special media.

Foul Odour

There were frequent complaints from the neighbourhood of E.T.P. about the four odours. Sometimes the odour was so intense that it was unbearable. When this was referred to the experts they were of the opinion that in the activated sludge process such odours are common. Levels for H_2S, Ammonia and Methane which are considered to produce foul odour were difficult to estimated in the Plant. The drying beds were inadequate and drying time was more than expected. We believe that the sludge removed from the clariflocculator which was not oxidized could be one of the cause. Frequent destabilization of the system also added to the odour problem.

After the expansion, destabilization of the plant is very less and there is no discharge into the drying beds from the clariflocculator since it has been converted into a thickner. The capacity of the drying beds was also increased. The sludge that is discharged into the beds was already oxidized and hence does not emit foul odour during drying.

Some Guidelines for Operation

By our experience we found that the following points may be helpful in monitoring the effluent treatment plant:

1. Colour of mix in the Aeration tanks when in operation should be brown. Turning towards Grey or Black indicates a possible destabilization of system shortly.
2. Excessive foaming in the aeration tanks indicates the high D.O. levels which may result in sludge carryovers if the D.O. level is not controlled by reducing the speed of the aerator or switching off one of the aerators.
3. Odour : The odour in the aeration tanks should be similar to Sea Shore smell. Any foul odour means the biomass require enriching.
4. A sample of return sludge or aeration tank mix when examined under microscope, should show the movement of microorganisms and protozoa. Absence of any movement indicates biomass is inactive. Discharge of more sludge into beds and less raw waste intake revives the system.
5. For any reason if the plant is shut off for more than on hour it is better to recirculate the whole system atleast for an hour before taking the fresh raw effluent into the system. This will bring the D.O.level to the optimum level and make the biomass active. Preferably the recirculation should be carried till the colour of mix in the aeration tanks changes to brown.

Chapter 17

Safety and Quality Assurance in Dairy Industry: A Case Study

P.N. Reddy
Head-Q.I. and P.D.,
Mother Dairy, Delhi – 110 092

Introduction

Milk is not as simple as it looks, it is a very complex substance. It contains Fat in emulsion, Protein in colloidal and Lactose in true solution forms. The minor components like Minerals and Vitamins are either in dissolved form are associated with the major constituents

It is a product man cannot synthesize in a Laboratory on a commercial scale.He can manipulate its original form into various acceptable forms. Sometimes overtaken by greed he adulterates which is a sin against society and punishable under law.

Innovation

Man discovered that milk spoils if he keeps it out – so he boiled milk which ultimately lead to pasteurization, sterilization techniques. He also found if the milk become sour it tastes different, appearance/ texture changes but relishable – only at a certain stage it becomes unfit to his taste. This has lead to the innovation of fermented foods which have therapeutic value.

Man also found that by keeping milk fat separates out and this milk fat can be kept for longer periods and used. This lead to the innovation of cream, butter and ghee.

As man started finding various edible foods he started mixing and preparing various foods containing milk with other foods leading to milk sweets (burfi, khoa, kheer, payasam, Ice creams etc).

Then came the vegetarian and non-vegetarian concept. To supplement a vegetarian with proteins, paneer and cheese came into existence.

From the above it is clear that MILK has taken different forms in our daily food. In whatever form it is made available to the consumer the product has to be of acceptable quality.

Quality Management

This refers to management systems involving all the stake holders in maintaining quality of the products and services offered by the industry.

- ✰ Does it means QUALITY refer to standards?
- ✰ Does it means QUALITY refer to composition?
- ✰ Does it means QUALITY refer to what consumer wants?

The last question appears to be answering the meaning of quality. Therefore, it is freshness, nutritious, pure, safe, no adverse effect on health, free from defects, easily available, affordable, serve with smile, well packed, information on the label, customer friendly, keep one fit and fine etc. To be simple quality means safe food.

Quality

Quality has been defined as "The totality of characteristics of an entity that bears on its ability to satisfy stated and implied needs".

The importance of quality can best be explained in the words of Sueo Yamaguchi, Consultant, JIPM: "Quality is not something to be discussed. In Japan it is not something you talk about. It should be there. That's all. That is how it should be in India too".

Quality Assurance at Mother Dairy

Mother Dairy follows a strict system of Quality Assurance in order to provide consumers with milk of high quality. The system begins with procurement. Poor quality milk is not accepted. Every batch of incoming milk is tested for fat, SNF, acidity, bacteriological quality and presence of preservatives or neutralisers which are not permitted by law. During processing various checks are kept to ensure quality of the product. After processing, the milk is again checked for bacteriological and keeping qualities, as well as fat and SNF contents in order to ensure that it meets the rigid standards.

In addition, daily checks on milk are carried out at the Dairy after every tanker has been loaded. The checks are repeated on their return. Spot checks are also made at retail outlets to ensure that the required quality standards are met. Besides product control, strict control is kept on sanitation, both at the plant and retail outlets. Chemical and bacteriological tests are conducted at various points to ensure equipments/products quality. The water of the Dairy is softened, chlorinated and regularly tested to maintain the highest standards. The quality of the water used at the booths and insulated containers is also checked and corrective measures are taken wherever necessary..

All the Quality Assurance activities were meticulously blended into Food Safety/HACCP System.

Food Safety at Mother Dairy (Milk Plant)

- ☆ What is safe food? Safe food is a food, which does not cause any harm or injury or disease when consumed by consumer.
- ☆ To ensure and assure safe food to the consumers, HACCP was developed as a tool, which is nothing but an assurance of wholesomeness and safety.
- ☆ Historically HACCP was first used as a process tool in 1960s by a Company in consultation with NASA (National Aeronautics and Space Administration) to ensure safe food for the astronauts.

Commitment of Management and Employees, GMP, GHP and GLP form the foundation for the following preliminary requirements of HACCP.

1. Assembling HACCP Team – HACCP Team is a multi skilled Team consisting of Specialist from different fields like microbiologist, chemist, technologists, engineer,

product specialist for developing an effective HACCP Plan. The Team Members were identified and assigned task of implementing HACCP at Mother Dairy.

2. Description of the product. – Product was described completely by the team and the team acquired complete knowledge of the product.
3. Identifying intended use – Use of the product was understood properly by the team (where, how and who will be using the product).
4. Construction of flow diagram – All the stages in the food chain from reception of raw materials, processing, storage and all other operations were put stepwise on a sheet of a paper.
5. On site confirmation of the flow diagram – HACCP Team visited the place where each step of the process was being carried out and confirmed the Flow Diagram.

Having carried out the preliminary steps the team started implementing seven HACCP principles.

I) Hazard analysis.
II) Determine the Critical Control Points (CCPs)
III) Establish critical limit (s).
IV) Monitor the CCP.
V) Establish the corrective actions.
VI) Procedure for verification
VII) Documentation.

Principle 1 – Hazard Analysis

☆ Hazard is nothing but an agent in food, which can cause an adverse health effect.

☆ Primarily, there are three basic food hazards, namely biological, physical and chemical.

☆ Relative risk of each hazard is assessed based on the probability of occurrence and its effect on the human health.

- In Milk, the biological hazards are bacteria/germs, virus, fungus etc which enter into the milk from the animal, environment, improperly cleaned equipments or if the milk is not stored properly (At refrigerated temperature)
- Physical hazards in milk could be dust/dirt, grass, hair or other foreign matter in the milk which finds its way in to the milk at village level. Since Mother Dairy is receiving milk from State Co-operative Milk Unions these hazards are taken care at the appropriate places.
- Contaminated water, soap/detergent solution used for cleaning of equipments, other natural contaminants or milk is adulterated intentionally constitutes the chemical hazards. The adulterants detection kit developed by NDDB and Mother Dairy is extensively used to control the menace of adulteration.
- This exercise was repeated at different steps in the process.

Principle 2 – Determine the Critical Control Points (CCPs)

- Having done a preliminary hazard analysis, the next step was to identify critical control points with the help of a series of intelligent questions.
- Critical Control Points is defined as a point where control is necessary for food safety.
- All significant hazards identified during hazard analysis are addressed
- In Mother Dairy, two Critical Control Points have been identified.
- One is pasteurization of milk and second is storage of milk (Pasteurization is a process where the milk is heated to a defined temperature and held at that temperature for a defined time and immediately cooled to less than 10°C. Heating is done to destroy all the pathogens, *i.e.* disease reducing micro organisms and most of the non-pathogenic but milk spoiling organisms to make milk safe for human consumption. Cooling is done to stop the growth of the remaining harmless bacteria.

Principle 3 – Establish Critical Limit(s)

- Once the critical control points are established the team determined the critical limits for preventive measures associated with each identified CCP.
- Critical limit is the point, which differentiate between safe and unsafe products. For each CCP, a critical limit is defined. Critical limit should be meaningful and realistic.
- At Mother Dairy, we use HTST (High Temperature Short Time) Pasteurizer for pasteurizing the milk. We specify pasteurization temperature (77 ± 2°C) and time 16 seconds. For storage of milk, we specify storage temperature (less than 7°C).

Principle 4 – Monitor the CCP

- Monitoring is a planned sequence of observation or measurement to assess whether a CCP is under control.
- Rapid Physical and Chemical test are preferred over lengthy microbiological test, which may take some time more than 48 hours.
- Basically action plan is made to monitor CCPs. It is specified in the plan what to monitor, how to monitor, who will monitor and when to is monitor.
- At Mother Dairy the time and temperature is monitored on Distributed Control System (DCS) continuously. Temperature is set at 77 ± 2°C and is controlled by PID (Proportionally Integrated Derivative) steam valve and diversion is set at 75°C.

Principle 5 – Establish the Corrective Actions

- If the critical limit is violated, then corrective action is instituted.
- Corrective actions are written procedures to be followed when a deviation occurs.
- The actions must ensure that the CCP has been brought under control.
- Corrective actions taken must be recorded.
- In case of milk processing, the critical control point was milk pasteurization temperature. If temperature drops less

than 75°C, milk is automatically diverted to balance tank for reprocessing.

- ☆ The confirmatory test for pasteurization is phosphates test. If this test is found positive the milk is reprocessed
- ☆ For the storage of milk, critical control point was the storage temperature. If the temperature during storage is found more than 7°C, which is the specified limit, the milk is further deep chilled using Glycol System during filling into tankers.

Principle 6 – Procedure for Verification

- ☆ Verification is a confirmation process that HACCP Plan is effectively and accurately implemented.
- ☆ Verification activity includes What, How, When and Who.
- ☆ Each batch of pasteurized milk is tested for phosphatase test before it is released for filling into tankers for dispatch. Only batches passing the test are taken for filling.
- ☆ Frequency of verification at Mother Dairy is once a month to conform that the HACCP system is working effectively.
- ☆ Verification is also done by HACCP Certifying Agency once a year.

Principle 7 – Documentation

- ☆ Efficient and accurate record keeping is essential to the application of HACCP system.
- ☆ HACCP procedures should be documented *i.e.* Hazard Analysis, CCP determination, critical limit etc.
- ☆ It includes all related processing records, monitoring records and corrective action records, HACCP check list etc.
- ☆ All the records related to HACCP in Mother Dairy are stored in Computer.

Conclusion

HACCP is a science based systematic approach to food safety to provide safe food to customers.

It requires top management commitment and a dedicated team.

For HACCP to be effective, the people responsible for it need to be competent. Hence training becomes the single most important element in setting up a HACCP System. Training should provide the technical skill to implement the HACCP and help in changing the attitude of people.

Mother Dairy is Accredited with ISO-9002, HACCP and ISO-14001 from BVQI and the laboratory by NABL Certification which clearly shows all the Management Systems are of International Standards.

Quality Assurance and Food Safety is not only about protecting the consumer, but doing business profitably in and around the world.

Chapter 18

Present Status of Traditional Dairy Products

G.S. Rajorhia

(Ex- Principal Scientist NDRI)

154 Sector-7, Urban State, Karnal – 132 001, Haryana

Introduction

Nearly half of the 90 million tones of milk produced in India is utilized for the manufacture of a variety of traditional milk products. Most of these products are produced on a small scale either in villages or by h*alwais* in the cities and towns. Production centers are located in various pockets near big cities. The studies on the cost of production of some selected traditional products at these centers have shown good profitability. Besides being lucrative, the technologies used are simple with low operating and over head costs as compared with Western or European style products. A number of technological and social benefits can be attributed to indigenous milk products.

The art of preparing sweets from surplus milk was developed centuries ago. Lack of cooling facilities to keep liquid milk fresh in warm climate resulted in the diversion of milk for the preparation of indigenous milk products with comparatively longer shelf life. Milk food delicacies are value added products generating high profit. The demand for milk sweets is influenced by the nutritional and social value attached to each of them. In view of the growing awareness towards the safety aspects of milk based sweets in Indian cities and towns, the consumer shall prefer to buy these products from the organized establishments with a given brand. For this reason, some dairy plants are seeking information on technology of indigenous sweets.

The organized dairies at present handle and process about 12-15 per cent of the total milk produced in India. Collection of the entire surplus milk from about 5.8 lakh villages and its processing would require huge capital investment on equipment, building and other infra structure. The milk supplies in the cities and towns become very expensive as a result of high cost of procurement, processing and packaging and accompanying sourage losses. The large size dairy plants usually work on low throughput. Conversion of milk into indigenous milk products in and around milk production areas would be least expensive and more remunerative because of the simple technologies, use of low grade energy sources, inexpensive infra structure, local availability of equipment and low production costs as compared with other system of dairy processing. Indigenous milk products offer several technological and social benefits, generate employment, increase income and improve the economic status of the masses. Although authentic statistical data are not available, it may be estimated that about 45 million tons of milk is converted into traditional products annually in India.

Traditional Milk Products in Ancient India

Milk and milk products formed the principal ingredient of food of Vedic Indians. Khoa sweets have been the item of choice for centuries in India. In early Buddhist and Jain works, there is a mention that the sweets were prepared from inspissated milk named as *Sihakesara* and *Morandeka.* It appears that the rich used to enjoy such delicacies at the end of their meals. Buddha allowed his followers to take some sweets for journeys on routes where it was difficult to get food stuffs. In the Maurya period the sweets were prepared from concentrated milk with the addition of honey, jaggery or sugar. In the post –Gupta period (AD 750 to 1200), milk was used in various forms. When half of the quantity was evaporated, it was drunk. In case it was reduced to one third of the original quantity, it became a dish that was appreciated. When one-sixth of the original quantity remained, it was used for preparing sweets and when only one-eighth remained, it was called 'Sarkara' (powder). The ancient medical literature clearly states that the physical and mental happiness of individual depended on the food they took.

The art of preparing sweets from surplus milk was developed centuries ago. Lack of cooling facilities for liquid milk especially in warm climate resulted in the diversion of milk for the preparation of indigenous milk products with a view to achieve longer shelf-life.

Economic Importance of Indigenous Products

Milk food delicacies are value added products generating high profits. The demand for milk sweets is influenced by the nutritional and social value attached to each of them. In view of the growing awareness towards the safety aspects of milk based sweets in Indian cities and towns, the consumers would prefer to buy these products from the organized establishment. For this reason, many dairy plants are demanding information on technology of indigenous milk sweets. A critical review on the subject highlighting the weaknesses of the available technologies and the need for developing commercial production systems for each of the products will be presented.

Range of Indigenous Milk Products

Tables 18.1 and 18.2 represent the kind of traditional milk products which are prepared in India. This list is not exhaustive as many region specific products are made at different place and they do not find place here.

Table 18.1: Common Traditional Indian Milk Products

Process	*Product*	*Western Counterpart*
Concentration	Khoa	Evaporated milk
By evaporation	Basundi	Sweetened condensed milk
	Rabri	Sweetened clotted cream
	Khurchan	
	Malai	
Coagulation by	Chhana	Direct acidified cheese
heat and acid	Paneer	Latin American white cheese
Fermentation with lactic	Dahi	Plain yoghurt
acid bacteria	Payodhi	Sweetened-Yoghurt

Contd...

Table 18.1–Contd...

Process	*Product*	*Western Counterpart*
	Misti beverage	Concentrated and caramelized Sweet yoghurt
	Chakka	Drained yoghurt
	Srikhand	——
	Srikhand wadi	——
	Lassi, Chhach	Stirred yoghurt
Phase inversion of fat	Makkhan	Butter
	Malai/loni	
Butter classification	Ghee	Butter oil
Freezing	Kulfi	Ice-cream and other frozen deserts
	Kulfa	
	Malai-ka-baraf	

The list of most common milk sweets and novelties prepared by combining one or more of the above indigenous milk products with non-dairy ingredients is given in Table 18.2.

Table 18.2: Some Milk Based Delicacies

Khoa Based	*Chhana Based*	*Cereal Based*
Variety of Burfi	Rasogolla and varieties	Kheer
Peda	Sandesh and varieties	Paysam
Kalakand	Pantoa, Lady Caning	Phirni
Gujhia	Raso-Malai	Mihidana
Palangtod	Cham-Cham	Kadhi
Malai-Laddoo	Ksheer-Sagar	Ras-kheer
Kunda/Dudh pak	Rajbhog	
Milk-Cake	Sita-bhog	
Gulabjamun	Chhana-murki	
Kalajam		
Carrrot-Halwa	Chhana-kheer (porridge)	
Gourd-Halwa	Lalmohan	
Malpooa	Totapuri	
	Chitrakut	

Present Status of Indigenous Products

Variations in Composition

The small traders and Halwais, except for about 20 per cent of total ghee contributed by the organized dairy plants, produce the indigenous milk products. The traditional methods are good for cottage scale, but do not permit efficient utilization of fuel. These processes are labour intensive. The quality of products varies in respect of moisture, texture and flavour. The quality of milk used, degree of heat treatment, manner of handling of products and duration and condition of storage lead to variations in the chemical composition, beyond normal statistical limits near two batches of same products prepared at the shop would match in proximate principle, not to speak about the large variation between the shops, standardization of techniques for uniform quality is necessary.

Unhygienic Conditions

The unhygienic conditions at the production unit lead to contamination of products with different types of microorganisms leading to a low shelf life of the base products. This problem gets aggravated during summer in respect of composition, microbiological quality, sensory properties and shelf life. A variety of micro-organisms comprising of millions of *mesophiles*, acid producers, spore formers, *coliforms*, *staphylococci*, yeast and moulds per gm can be found in the products.

Inadequate Packaging

Most of the products are sold in the market without proper packaging and unduly exposing them to atmospheric contamination. It is, therefore, not feasible to lay down any microbiological standards for these products.

Sensory Quality Differences

Ghee is the most important indigenous milk product utilizing nearly 29 per cent of total milk. Although it is a long life product, it has typical sensory problems. There are examples of market ghee being adulterated with vegetable fats, lard, tallow, etc. According to a survey of the leading ghee trading centers in the Northern India, it was observed that even the most selling branded ghee were deficient in one way or the other. The flavour defects reported by the trended panel of judges in the ghee samples collected from the market are given in Table 18.3.

Table 18.3: Sensory Defects in Market Samples of Ghee

Total Samples	96
Oxidized flavour	29
Rancid flavour	10
Smoky flavour	12
Fruity flavour	02
Burn/Cooked flavour	18
Bland or lacking flavour	09
Curdy/acidic flavour	06
Good normal flavour	10

Texture defects were also observed in the market samples of ghee the peroxide value in the above samples ranged between 0.0 and 12.72 as meq. Of oxygen per kg of fat and 0.04 to 2.0 per cent moisture. Other constants were within the prescribed limits.

Modernization and Upgradation of Technologies

Industrial methods have now been developed for mechanized production, packaging and storage of khoa, chhana, ghee, dahi, gulabjamun, burfi, peda, rasogolla, kalakand and shrikhand. These products are being produced regularly on a factory scale. Many of these products are stored and transported in refrigerated cabinet and packaged in food grade plastic containers.

The production of traditional milk products by using modern methods would promote the utilization of larger quantities of milk during the flush season and help in stabilization of milk prices. With the help of recombined milk technology, traditional milk products can also be produced in lean months and in the milk deficient zones. Technology for recombined milk products is available for industrial application.

The recent developments in convenience traditional milk products category like khoa powder, rasogolla, mix powder, gulabjamun mix powder, kulfi mix powder, chhana powder, shrikhand powder, etc with prolonged shelf-life and high consumer acceptability have supported the modernization efforts of this sector to a great extent.

Marketing of Indigenous Products

The demand for traditional products far exceeds that of western type dairy products. The increasing requirements for these products present a great opportunity for organized dairies to modernize production. However, most of these products because of high water activity, are perishable at room temperature. A provision of cold chain will, therefore, be necessary to preserve the traditional products for long periods. Maintenance of uniform quality throughout will promote marketing. Milk sweets sold by *halwais* at exorbitant rates are reported to carry abnormally high microbial load besides being substandard in chemical and textural properties. Since the children, are more prone to diseases and they are biggest consumer of milk based sweets, this reason alone should greatly favour the manufacture and marketing of indigenous milk products through organized channels. Effective packaging is yet another consideration for good marketing strategies. The products manufactured in the area of plentiful milk availability, especially during flush season, can be marketed in the places of milk scarcity and in urban areas, where milk is a scarce product and expensive because of high transportation cost. Milk sweets with well defined quality characteristics and packaged in attractive containers can be marketed at parlours, milk booths, hostels and restaurants, departmental canteens, supermarkets, airlines and railways catering, hostels and other points of strategic nature.

Future Directions

The need for up grading the technology for production, packaging, preservation and distribution of indigenous milk products is greatly realized now. Attempts to develop any large scale processes for milk based sweets must aim at using the already existing process in food plant rather than relying on a new plant design and fabrication which carry limitation of available engineering skill, high cost and time loss. In view of the growing market demands for indigenous milk products and their derivatives, there is a great scope for adopting the existing unit process technologies for industrial production. Many new processes such as membrane technology for concentration of milk have been recommended in the recent past. There is a considerable scope for using process for conserving regional and seasonal milk surpluses. The chemical and microbiological changes during storage and transportation diminish both the nutritional quality and consumer's acceptance of milk sweets. High ambient temperatures and relative humidity greatly contribute to the spoilage problem. A good possibility exists for improving the shelf-life of milk sweets by employing few of the selected approaches such as modified atmospheric or vacuum packaging, use of humectants and natural preservatives and adherence to good manufacturing practices. The quality of raw milk, of course, is of paramount importance for producing high-grade milk products. Enforcement of standard sanitary practices at all stages of products handling, packaging and distribution will boost marketing and lead to heavy dividends. Quality assurance in terms of food safety and freedom from contamination is desired to be achieved. Risk assessment during milk production and processing must receive priority is dairy research and education in India to become globally competitive.

Chapter 19

Recent Advances in the Manufacture of Khoa

G.S. Rajorhia
Principal Scientist,
D.T. Division, NDRI, Karnal

Introduction

Khoa, prepared by open pan evaporation of milk serves as a base for a variety of Indian sweets, *e.g.*, burfi, peda, gulabjamun, etc. The traditional khoa manufacturing practices suit the small scale operation. The process is labour and energy intensive. The sensory, chemical and microbial qualities of market samples of khoa were not adequately characterized in the past. Studies were, therefore, conducted to evaluate the quality of khoa marketed in major cities of India and to explore the possibilities of large scale production and mechanization of khoa making with enhanced shelf-life.

Quality of Market Khoa

A large variation in quality of market khoa samples was observed. Three major varieties of khoa, *viz.*, *Pindi*, *Dhap* and *Danedar* are sold in the Indian markets. The chemical composition, sensory characteristics and the end uses of each variety are found to be different. On the basis of these findings, the Bureau of Indian Standards was advised to revise the khoa standard, incorporating the distinguishing characteristics of the three varieties. Since khoa is prepared at boiling temperature, it should be a sterile product. However, market samples of khoa were heavily contaminated with acid producing, proteoiytic, lipolytic, sporulating and chromogenic type bacteria, besides yeast and moulds, coliforms and staphylococci. The unhygienic practices of handling of product after its preparation are responsible for inferior quality of market samples.

Physico-Chemical Changes During Manufacture of Khoa

The various physico-chemical and biochemical changes occurring during the manufacture and storage of khoa have been studied. The investigations were extended to basic chemistry of protein to correlate denaturation. Lactose, fat, minerals and vitamins as influenced by progressive concentration during manufacture and subsequent storage of khoa. The effects of kind and quality of milk on the sensory, chemical and rheological properties of khoa were thoroughly investigated. Useful recommendations have been made to utilise various types of milk for khoa making on differential basis.

Process Innovations for Khoa Making

A number of approaches, alternative methods and materials for industrial production of khoa were tried. A brief account of the findings suitable for large scale adoption by the dairy plants is given hereunder:

Use of Vacuum Concentrated Milk

Moisture removal is the key operation in the manufacture of khoa. Khoa making in the open pan at atmospheric pressure is energy wise expensive requiring approximately 455 kcal of energy per kg of milk. Thus, it became imperative to develop low energy processes for khoa making. In pursuance of this objective, studies were conducted to evolve a suitable technology based on the utilization of vacuum concentrated milk for khoa making. The facilities vacuum for concentration and drying of milk are available in the dairy plants manufacturing milk products.

Using a multiple effect evaporator, cow's and buffalo's milks were concentrated to 31 and 40 per cent total solids, Khoa samples prepared from concentrated milk with 31 per cent TS were comparable with the control samples in respect of chemical composition and organoleptic properties. Use of milk with 40 per cent solids produced khoa which had flat flavour and sticky texture. It was calculated that preconcentration of milk from 15 to 31 per cent solids before khoa making consumed less than half the energy (209 kcal/kg of milk) of that required by open pan merhod. Based on these reports, many commercial dairies now use the concentrated milk for khoa making.

Use of RO Concentrated Milk

A process has been developed for the manufacture of khoa using reverse osmosis for pre-concentration of milk. Khoa manufactured from RO concentrated whole milk (31 per cent TS) was comparable in flavour and texture with conventional product. The energy consumption in RO concentration was estimated to be about 80 kcal/kg of milk for batch process and 25 kcal for continuous process which brings about a net saving of 335 to 430 kcal/kg of milk.

Use of Dried Milk for Khoa Making

Although satisfactory quality khoa was obtained from roller dried whole milk, the spray powders reconstituted to 65 per cent total solids yielded the product which lacked the characteristic nutty flavour. Reconstitution of whole milk powder to less than 40 per cent total solids was necessary to prolong the heating time for unmasking the sulphydryl groups so as to increase the intensity of cooked flavour and to release the free fat to avoid stickiness.

Adoption of Roller Drying Process for Khoa Making

Atmospheric roller dryers which were hitherto used for the manufacture of milk powders in past, have been replaced by the spray dryers in the dairies. Many of the existing roller dryers are lying idle. Attempts were, therefore, made to examine the feasibility of preparing khoa on the roller dryers by adjusting the process variables such as steam pressure, roller speed, degree of concentration of milk, flow rate of the concentrated milk and manipulating the distance between the rollers and the scraping blades. Vacuum concentrated milk with 50 per cent total solids preheated to 74°C for 10 min was found suitable for khoa making on roller dryers at 25–30 psi. A kneader is placed at the outlet of the roller drier to make a homogeneous mass of khoa.

Chapter 20

Venturing in Dairy Industry

Rajendra K. Pandey
Head, Department of Animal Husbandry and Dairying, Institute of Agricultural Sciences, Banaras Hindu University, Varanasi – 221 005

In order to understand what sustainable development means one need to make a distinction between growth and development. Growth is a quantitative increase coming mainly from the assimilation of products or of the incomes, while development is a qualitative change in the life of human being visible in their use of material goods, in their standard of living, in their education and in their prosperity our conventional method of estimating the growth is through GDP- that is Gross Domestic Products or through Gross National Products (GNP).

Every country produced a number of commodities and service. Each one of these can be assigned a value, and when we assimilate all these values, it becomes the gross domestic products. In the conventional method of estimating GDP, there is no concern for the improvement of life that has taken place. All these conventional method have a drawback that they do not take into account the loss of natural resources in the production process, either renewable or non-renewable, is utilized. But, in the conventional method, there is no account taken of the resources which are lost in the production process of these commodities. So we may be having a higher growth rate, but in fact it may not the adding to any development. Does the economic development lead to better human beings? Does the economic growth lead to better life on this planet for human beings. The answer is 'No'. We know of the contradictions, the great disparities that the economic growth has brought in this world. Today billions of people are living below the poverty line. Thousands of young children die daily due to malnutrition and diseases. One third of the world's adult population lives in India. Half of them are illiterate, two-third of them being women. Income wise also there are great disparities in the world. The rich of the world, per cent of what is poorest one-fifth of the world could take out. The industrialized nation consumes 10 times more energy than the developing nations. Also 70 per cent of the total waste and the emissions from the harmful oxides and other gases are discharged by the developed nations. So, has the economic growth really brought about any improvement in the living standards of the nations, particularly the poor ones.

In such a contradiction situation, what is the meaning of sustainable development? Why should we talk about sustainable development at all? The answer is because we have come to realize that economic growth itself is not going to solve the problems of the world. It is not going to attack poverty prevailing in the world. It is only through sustainable development that we can tackle the problem of poverty. The duty imposed by sustainability on us is that we should replace the natural endowment of the world. The natural endowments of the world are non-renewable resources, like various types of plants, animals, livestock and other species. In our attempt to achieve higher and higher economic growth we should not forget that these natural endowments are the means which will provide a better living to the coming generations. It is our duty that each generation leaves behind, each generation replaces what it takes away from nature so that the future generation can have a similar or a better living standards.

Indian Dairy Industry and Sustainability

In the light of these criteria, let us examine the scenario of the dairy industry in India. Indian Agriculture is an economic symbiosis of crop and cattle production. Small and marginal farmers own almost 80 per cent of the total land holdings. About 67 per cent of the workfare of 280 million is engaged in agriculture either as cultivator or farm labour. In a normal year, crop production can generate employment for this work force for only 90 to 120 days. For the remaining period, they are virtually unemployed. In this milieu, dairying sets right these imbalances in employment. The dairy sector today provides some 70 million farm families the triple benefits of nutritive food, supplementary income and productive employment for family labour, mainly women, clearly, any effective programme for poverty alleviation would be strengthened by dairying.

Thus the first unique characteristic of Indian Dairy Industry is that it is in the hands of small holders. Two third of the milk producers are small or marginal farmers, 20 per cent of the milk producers have no land, 66 per cent of them have land, but they are small or marginal farmers with land holdings of a couple of hectares. For fodder requirements of their cattle, the Indian farmers mainly depend on the agricultural waste and agricultural by-products, or on grazing. They do not utilize grains, thus the cattle do not compete with the human beings. This is one of the distinct features of the Indian dairy industry and different from the industry related world where dairying in primarily based on the utilization of the import which compete with the requirements of human being.

The second feature of the Indian Dairy Industry is that because milk production by small farmers they keep one or two milch animals only. Therefore, the collection of small quantities of milk from these farmers is a very cumber some process. This was the reason why these milk producers were organized into a cooperative society.

Cooperative milk industry has many challenges. Some are internal others are external. The intensity of these challenges is on the increase due to the open industrial policy. The main challenge is to face the private industry. Cooperatives have to go through the numerous hurdles of rules and regulations. To have to go through the rituals of following all these rules on the one side and to compete in business with the private sector which is immune to all the provisions of law is a Herculean task.

Moving Towards Sustainable Dairy Industry

The rural financial growths of this country during the last more than four decades have deep roots in the cooperative movement. In Gujrat, dairying prospered out of the farmers strong felt need to cooperatives. The milk procurement, processing products, and the marketing operations have a well-knit network. Against this an

Indian milk producer has the orthodox thinking and vision since pre-independence day and he considered as animals are required for farming and manure is a good fertilizer. This resulted in, nominal milk production because there was no emphasis on improved breed of animals. Due to limited income from farming, the poor farmer had to deprive his children and family of the milk produced at home and sells it for making few more rupees. Marginal land-holding and lack of technical knowledge about the milk production were his other difficulties. However, his nominal income from milk proved to be a good support which has culminated in the cooperatives.

Cooperative Dairying

Collection of milk from all individual milk producers in the cooperative village level society and transporting it to the district level milk processing plant is a methodology adopted in the cooperative dairying. In the past or even today also in the caster region, the milk production was fully dependent on the middlemen or an agent visiting the village for buying the milk. If this did not happen for any reason milk being perishable, the only choice left to the producers was to consume in his household and convert the excess into butter and ghee by employing the traditional or crude methods those were known to him. These products were sold at throw away price. In contrast to this, today the milk producers is part of a national milk grid and of the latest technology and scientific way of milk production and processing.

Unfortunately, there is a general notion that milk is almost a free commodity, meaning the animals are free and the countryside grass is free. People conveniently forget that animal itself costs several thousand of rupees. Cost of rearing is not taken into account. Cost of feed and other inputs are overlooked.

Thus, sustainability is determined by the complex interaction of the biological physical and socio-economic factors that constitute the basis of all production systems. Sustainability should be treated as a dynamic concept making allowances for the changing need of steadily increasing global population. This requires a comprehensive approach to improve existing systems and to develop novel ones to avoid obsolescence. Expanding on this, it is not difficult to identify the four basic structures of dairy industry; in fact, these are common to most industries. The four structures are – production of milk, processing of milk, the consumer and human resources, what have been discussed above.

Thus, the Dairying is important for India as, it is rural based land saving and gender neutral. Compared to crop production, it has small favorable ratio of employment to output. Dairy farming makes a substantial source of income for the landless labour as well as the marginal farmers. It is scaled neutral and dominated by small herd sizes of two to four animals.

Cattle and buffaloes are integral part of mixed farming system that is typical of small holder agricultural systems. Dairy animals directly provide valuable inputs into our farm production activities and they function as important converters of crop residues into essential nutrition for whole community, especially for growing children with immediate beneficial impact on quality of life. India has emerged as the number one milk producers in the world and there are further great future scopes of progress in dairy sector in the rural development in the country. In the last 25 years, country has moved from a situation of scarcity and rationing of milk to a scenario which infuses considerable confidence in pushing ahead. Dairying is a sure path and future of our rural development.

Milk production in the country over the last two decade has increased by about 5 per cent per annum and the per capita availability of milk improved from 107 grams in 1970 to 214 grams at present. The per capita availability of milk has been increasing at a rate faster than the rate of increase of our population. Added to this growth rate in the fact that the cost of milk production in India is low as inputs are largely the by-products of the main agricultural activity. Not only is that most of the milk produced by labour houses in the margin. There is also a larger and rising domestic demand both for milk as well as for milk products. With an expanding middle income group, there even exist a market for value added products especially among quite a large segment of our population living in our cities and towns. There is also a possibility of converting surplus milk into unconventional milk products like casein and lactose which are not only import substitutes but also have a larger potential for export to developed countries. Modern scientific processing technology and managerial innovations being through about by our dairy managers are opening up before us opportunities of processing and marketing various types of value added milk and milk products.

Milk is consumed not only as a source of nutrition for our health but also, as products like, flavoured milk, various kinds of yoghurts, ice-cream, sweets and such other delicacies which would give larger price return to the industry and the milk producers as well. The emerging consumption pattern offered new challenges for the dairy industry, whereas various milk scheme has so far used to rationing the distribution of milk and milk products. Thus, the outlook of strategies is shifting from distribution to sales and marketing, opening up vast opportunities for the dairy industry.

The elasticity of demand for food grains being less than one, the impact of higher growth rate of income would result in shifts is household consumption. Milk and milk products would be one of the leading beneficiaries of increased consumption. In countries like China, where per capita income growth has been 9 per cent since last a decade, the demand for milk and meat recorded phenomenal increases. If income distribution does not become adverse to the poor, it is likely that the possibility of export of dairy products might hold higher potential than export of food grains. Since the milk production is different from many other agricultural per suits for reasons of extreme perishable nature of raw products, bulkiness and the biological process of continuous production, the gestation period which is a biological lag in output creates unique conditions and problems in handling milk production. Extreme perishability of milk and possibilities of contamination necessitates rapid movement of the product. The highly decentralized nature of the production asset, namely the milch cow and buffalo and the less than adequate development of physical infrastructure makes the desired speed of movement of milk difficult. The specially scattered nature of production brings up face to face with the problems of collection and transportation especially in linking remote villages with the market centres. Improvements in the organization to collect, process and distribute milk will reduce spoilage and dampen the seasonal variation in prices and there by expand the effective market for milk. Effort in breed improvement and genetic improvement through use of bio-technology and embryo transfer technology have kindled hopes of substantial increase in milk yields. Longer lactation periods and shorter calving intervals, organized milk collection, establishment of chilling centres, availability of laboratory equipments and others measures have great potential to reduce our milk procurement time and enhance the life of raw milk thereby minimizing the wastage.

The dairy processing industry itself undergoing in process of diversification and expansion, the structure of dairy industry is under a change consequent to the de-licensing of the industry and the economic liberalization process. The role of the private sector is expanding especially in those areas where there is a marketable surplus beyond the carrying capacity of the existing cooperative infrastructure. De-licensing has brought in many new players in the field and is leading to expansion of capacities licensed in the past. There are proposals from the private industry to enter into manufacture of industrial products like lactose and casein. Some of them have already entered into collaboration with foreign companies. The base of the industry is thus expanding.

The above process of expansion of the industry and the diversification of the structural industry needs to he matched with the corresponding increase in the production base, namely the production of raw milk. The dairy farming will remain substantially as an adjunct to agriculture sustained largely on crop-by-products and residues. The lack of empirical data makes it difficult to correctly assess the size class of producers. However, the size distribution of dairy farming may also need to undergo some change towards larger herd sizes. Dairy farming has to emerge as an economic enterprise in itself. Even while the preponderance of the total milch population may continue to be an integral adjunct of the agricultural production process, the growth in herd size almost is natural out growth of advancement in dairying as has been experience of the developed countries. Such a growth will promote generation of employment for educated youth and can attract them into dairy farming as a profession.

Anand pattern and Operation Flood ventured into hither to un-chartered quarters. It is not that the cooperative form of association was not unknown, but it remained an ideology and some one had to come forward with the tools for translating it into action. Dr. Kurien performed the role of the messiah and demonstrated how a good ideology holding in it the basic tenets of democracy would also be an equally good and powerful method of action. Thus, an ideological package was transformed into a meaningful package for running an economic enterprise, namely a cooperative society. The commitment to sustain the cooperative as a business enterprise, while at the same time ensuring its democratic functioning and member participation gave us a shining example of how small individual efforts could through a medium of cooperative can become the ideal form of economic enterprise for rural development. The fact that the Anand model can be replicated has also been fairly well established. The model has given us the strength to induct high yielding milch animals among our small, marginal farmers and to organize processing and marketing of milk output so created, thereby building a vibrant and vertically integrated cooperative structure that can withstand the fluctuations of the market.

There are vast areas still uncovered by the meaningful program of increase in productivity and organized efforts for opening up market channels. India has extensive geographical terrains coming under wide range of agro-climatic conditions with rainfall ranging from say 100 mm to as much as 4000 mm. A large part of our agriculture development is confined to the irrigated areas which constitute some 30 per cent of our total cultivated land. Innovative methods of rain harvesting and moisture retention in the soil are slowly giving rise to a sustainable scenario of rain-fed agriculture.

Fodder cultivation and grassland development will be absorbed as important components of development of a water-shed. A lot of animal resource development has taken place in irrigated agriculture and, therefore, potential areas for future perhaps may be the lower rainfall areas where dairying will also serve drought proofing. Thus economic development comes through being together. Can there be a better togetherness than being together with the economic prosperity of small farmers, marginal farmers and landless labourers. If they can produce 60 per cent of the milk output, by 75 per cent of membership of milk producers' cooperatives, this togetherness deserves to be strengthened.

International Scenario

Till now the increase in milk production has been attained not because of the enhanced productivity of the animals, but due to the increase in number of animals. Also, the increase in the proportion of buffalo's milk as compared to the cow's milk has contributed to the overall enhanced milk production. The dominance of buffalo milk in our total milk production has put India on altogether different platform in the international context, because the international areas are characterized by the dominance of cow's milk. There is greater flow of milk from the rural area to the urban areas, because of the urban-rural income disparities. The law of gravitation would show that since the urban income is growing as a faster pace than the rural income, therefore, the greater flow of milk is taking place from the rural areas to the urban areas. As a result, there is aggregate demand which is kept unfulfilled in the rural areas primarily because of the price incentives offered for supplying the milk to urban areas.

To explain this fact an example can be taken into account, that in Haryana which is a smaller state and where the cooperative dairy federation operates at much more shoe-string procurement and capacity utilization, 45 dairy plants have come up in the past decade. And all them have the urban markets of Delhi and Haryana. Haryana is one of the fastest growing urban conglomerates. Now this is the scenario number one.

Scenario number two which can again be painted clue from the rural urban dichotomy is that now the processing and distribution dimensions are going to play dominant roles, the dairy plants are divided into three sectors- First is a rural dairy which is predominately engaged in chilling operations, collection and them passing on to the feeder balancing plant or to a feeder plant. Second is the Union Dairy, and the third is the one which would predominantly be a processing dairy plant which is involved in manufacturing certain milk products. Now that is where the challenges lie before the Indian dairy sectors to compete the international arena. Here the distribution is one dimension which would have a predominant weight-age in our decision. Now the only way that can manage is by increasing the price to the consumer and reducing the share of the producer. That would be a challenge which is going to face and we have seen the consequences as problems in terms of capacity utilization and the whole chain will be disturbed.

Financing and Viability of Dairy Industry

There is need for the dairy industry to come out of legacy of the past and carve out its role in an environment of economic liberalization, policy deregulation and do away with the superfluous taxation, and legislation that were restricting the growth and development of the private and the co-operative dairy sectors particularly cooperative act. The industrial deregulation and opening up of the economic the procedure for appraisal monitoring and financing of all projects, including the dairy, are gradually becoming together and the customers who would tend to present proposals that are not viable would not find favour with the financers as the cost of capital is becoming expensive and therefore, it is necessary for the dairy industry to improve efficiency of utilization of all resources including money, machine and manpower. Further, it is urged for adoption of a new National Dairy Policy in which the private sector should be given adequate representation in participating and formulating such policies. The dairy industry to become financially viable it was necessary to improve the efficiency of all systems *viz.* milk production and collection, processing and product manufacture, marketing and distribution, and above all the manpower training institutions so as to produce skilled manpower and specialist in dairy industry.

Conclusion

Indian Dairy Industry is matchless in the world. It is emerging as a sunrise industry growing at a snail's pace unlike poultry industry and India is the world's largest milk producers with its lower per animal productivity till date. India produces 16 per cent the world milk production, under 20 per cent of which is processed. A unique feature of this industry is that over 50 per cent of the total milk production comes from the buffalo. It is unique in the sense that no where outside the South Asian region buffaloes are used as milch animals.

Buffaloes are India's milking machine that constitute less than 40 per cent of the bovine population, but contribute more than half of the total milk production. Albeit India has the largest cattle population most of them are non-descript animals, very poor in milk production. For a country like India having a population of 1.2 billion and availability per capita availability of milk would be woefully low-at 220 g. per day when it fulfills, the projected output of 9.0 million tones. Available data indicate that the average milk intake is as paltry as 20 g/day in eastern region as against a high of 400 g/day in the north India. In northern belt, majority of the people are lacto vegetarians, they compensate the non consumption of chicken, eggs, meat and even fish through milk consumption. Milk production of northern belt is much higher than eastern and south eastern region.

The dairy industry is much older than poultry sector and it is a rural based activity spread widely across the country in some 70 million households rearing one or two cows/buffaloes. Not with standing the poor productivity of native cattle, India has emerged as the world's number one milk producing country. The average lactational milk yield of cows and buffaloes is 445 kg and 911 kg, respectively. So, Dairying has now emerged as an important income generating and a source of employment opportunities in rural areas.

Thus the dairy industry has developed enormously with the milk production more than trebling in the last few decades. Nevertheless stile there need a long way to go to achieve the true potential that the country has. Generation of new technologies for landless group of livestock owners, an efficient inputs supply and services and linkage between different channels of production and marketing management systems are however urgently required in the years to come.

India has a great potential to dairy industry with its products exports. India's low cost milk will be price competitive in milk deficit countries *viz.* surrounding India. Asia is the world's fastest growing market for dairy products. According to an F.A.O. expert, "India is the slumbering giant of the international dairy trade. India has the largest bovine population 206 million cattle and 814 million buffaloes which indicate the bright future of dairy industry".

Chapter 21

Application of ISO 9001 and HACCP for Improvement of Quality and Safety of Indigenous Dairy Products

Sohrab

Chief Executive,

Quality Care and International Consultant to UNESCAP

Introduction

India has achieved the distinction of being the largest milk producer in the world. The present dairy industry set up represents a blend of public, cooperative and private dairies. Each segment has its own problems and potentials. If dairy industry is to survive in the ever increasing global competition and excelling in its quality and safety approach, it has to seriously think of reorienting the paradigm of change. The change that encapsulates sound hygienic norms, good manufacturing practices, proactive food safety programme and quality management systems.

Processing of indigenous dairy products to satisfy the palate of the consumer is not enough. It must produced under hygienic environment and be free from harmful additives, microbial contamination, physical and chemical hazards and remain so for a period it is intended to be consumed. Therefore, the methods employed in quality assurance programmes will vary considerably in accuracy and sophistication according to the type of process and size and nature of resources available.

With the advent of Quality (ISO 9000) and Food Safety (HACCP) Management Systems, the concept of quality and food safety has taken a tangible form. For the first time there has been a broad consensus about quality and food safety system's minimum requirements. This is the reason why ISO 9000 has unanimously received a worldwide acceptance and HACCP is fast gaining momentum in its application. This presents a good opportunity for the dairy industry for upgrading quality and food safety and bringing uniformity and consistency in its products to domestic and international markets. These standards have become the subject of intense focus worldwide and are important both as a potential market place requirement and as a marketable company feature.

Since the International market has become demanding in terms of quality, safety and delivery, installation of quality and food safety have become *de rigueur* for long term survival and for entry into competitive domestic and global markets. The application of HACCP is compatible with the implementation of ISO 9000. The HACCP approach adds value to ISO 9000 Quality Management System and a combined effect of both would be a safe and wholesome indigenous dairy products to consumer.

The trade reforms initiated by the World Trade Organization (WTO) have already changed the business environment. The Technical Barriers to Trade (TBT) and Sanitary and Phytosanitary (SPS) agreements brought out under WTO govern the international trade. SPS is particularly applicable to food industry and adoption of HACCP standard under this agreement makes it mandatory for the food industry to apply Food Safety Management System (HACCP) for facilitating international trade.

Application of Quality Management Systems (ISO 9001:2000)

Quality a Moving Target

It would be relatively easy to determine the user's exact requirements at any given time and to conform to them. However, these requirements are not static. There are many forces at work such as statutory requirements, customer requirements, technological changes, fashion and competition. Therefore, customer perceptions of quality are constantly changing and new demands emerging.

Only the producers able to keep that consumer requirements constantly in their sights, and also meet it, will survive and grow, those who miss will gradually lose market share and disappear. There are many examples of such companies. Indigenous dairy product manufactures have major goals increasing profit, larger market share etc. None of these goals will be met if they do not find out what the customer wants and do not find ways of satisfying those customer needs.

The forwardlooking companies are determining those future needs now, so that they can come to the market before the competition. They bring products/services to the market, which have characteristics the current users are not even dreaming of, thereby moving the quality target yet again. The competition will have to, at least, match that quality or improve on it if it wishes to stay in that market place.

If there is too much emphasis in the business on pure 'conformance' rather than 'fitness for use' for purpose the business will not extend its frontiers and will stagnate. It follows then, that the dairy's resources, finances and processes should be established with a common purpose throughout the business. If there are parts of the business which are not contributing towards this purpose then their continued existence in that form must be questioned very closely.

Process Approach

The dairies therefore should pursue quality in the changing circumstances. Application of the concept of process approach, which has been developed by the International Organization for Standardization (ISO) through ISO 9001:2000 and very successfully used by organizations around the world, is the answer to current business scenario. It will follow that each functional department, each process within each department and every person within each of those processes must have a common understanding of the business's goals and their role within them. However each person, section and department does not work in isolation. Each is dependent on others for product and/or information; each is responsible for his/her job and is also responsible for providing an output, which is of use by someone else in the business.

The business therefore is made up of a myriad of small links whereby people receive information from each other, process it with each other and then send it to the next "processor", and so on. This concept is given many names but a well-known one is the PROCESS APPROACH by the ISO. It sees everyone in an organization as a customer, a processor and a supplier, *i.e.* three roles (Figure 21.1). As a customer each person receives a product and/or information from supplier(s); each person is responsible for processing this input *i.e.* doing their job right the first time and then passing that processed output to someone else which acts as their input. In the latter role it is as a supplier.

There is obviously no point in receiving and using input that is not fit for use so, as a customer, each person should discuss and agree with their supplier what is 'fit for use'. Having done that, the process must be set up and operated to minimize all the variables which could prevent the product being produced correctly first time.

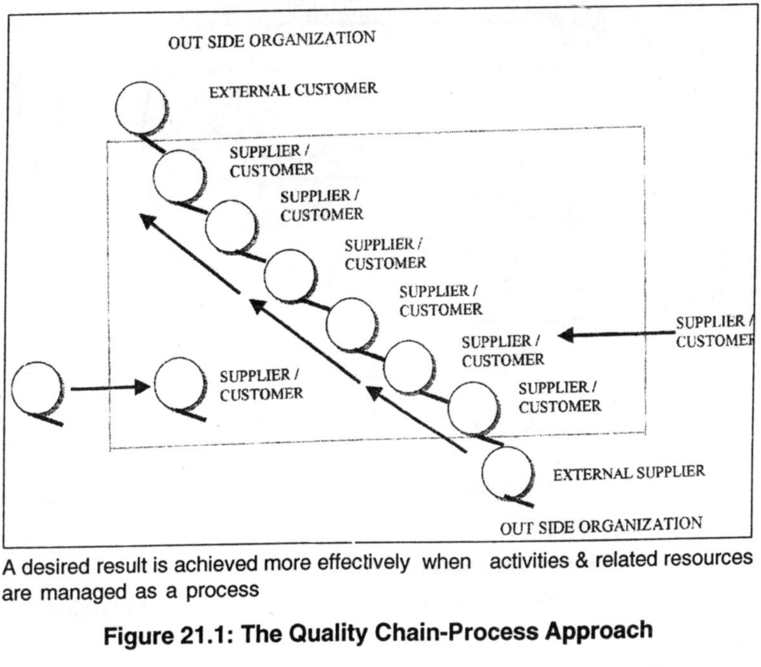

A desired result is achieved more effectively when activities & related resources are managed as a process

Figure 21.1: The Quality Chain-Process Approach

ISO 9001:2000: A Process Model

The model of a process-based quality management system shown in Figure 21.2 illustrates the process linkages presented in clauses 4 to 8 of the ISO 9001 standard. This illustration shows that customers play a significant role in defining requirements as inputs. Monitoring of customer satisfaction requires the evaluation of information relating to customer perception as to whether the organization has met the customer requirements. This model covers all the requirements of ISO 9001, but does not show processes at a detailed level.

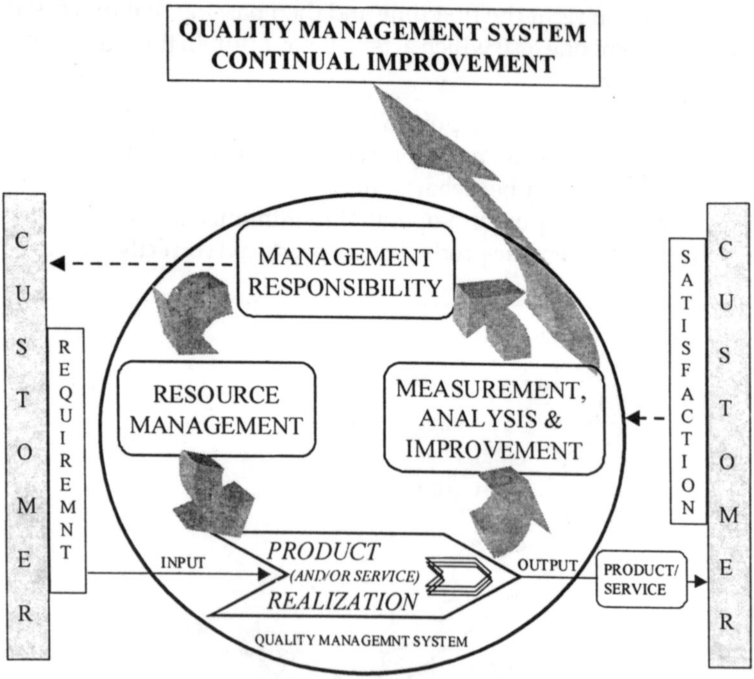

Figure 21.2: ISO 9000 Process Model

The model when used within a quality management system, emphasizes the importance of:

1. Understanding and meeting requirements,
2. The need to consider processes in term of added value,

3. Obtaining results of process performance and effectiveness, and
4. Continual improvement of processes based on objective measurement.

Inherent in this model is continual improvement cycle which is constantly at work with all processes. This is called Deming cycle after one of the outstanding Quality Gurus Dr. Deming or simply P-D-C-A cycle (Figure 21.3).

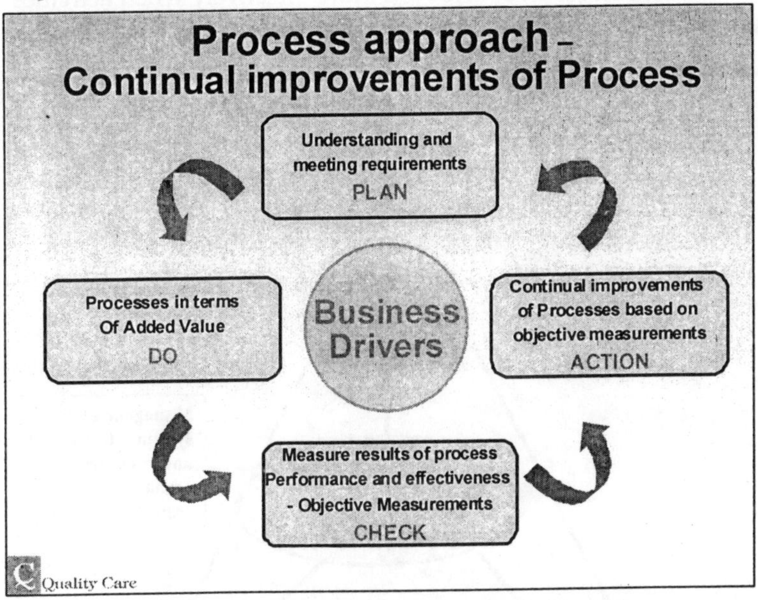

Figure 21.3: P-D-C-A Cycle or Deming Cycle

ISO 9000 as Driver for Process Management

This International Standard specifies requirements for a quality management system applicable to all industries such as software, hardware, process material and services which is composed of three words Quality-Management-systems (Figure 21.4). In this model an organization :

1. Needs to demonstrate its ability to consistently provide product that meets customer and applicable regulatory requirements, and

2. Aims to enhance customer satisfaction through the effective application of the system, including processes for continual improvement of the system and the assurance of conformity to customer and applicable regulatory requirements.

A complete synergy among the quality parameters, systems and management provides a better performance when applied as management system.

A desired result is achieved more effectively when activities and related resources are managed as a process, ISO 9000 Quality

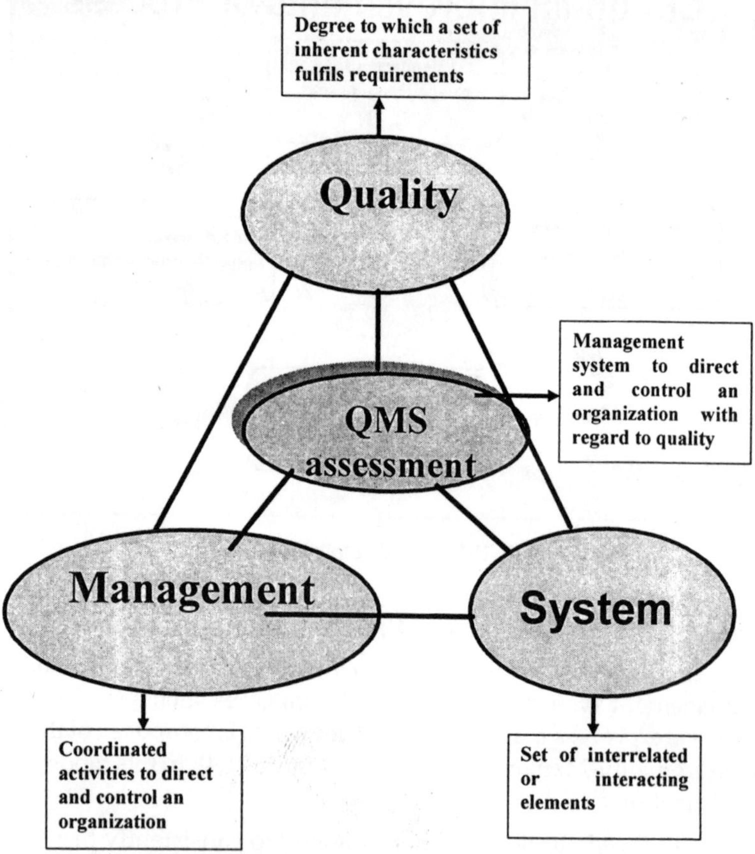

Figure 21.4: Linkages Between Quality-Management and System Elements

Management System Standard advocates application of process in the operation of process model (Figure 21.5).

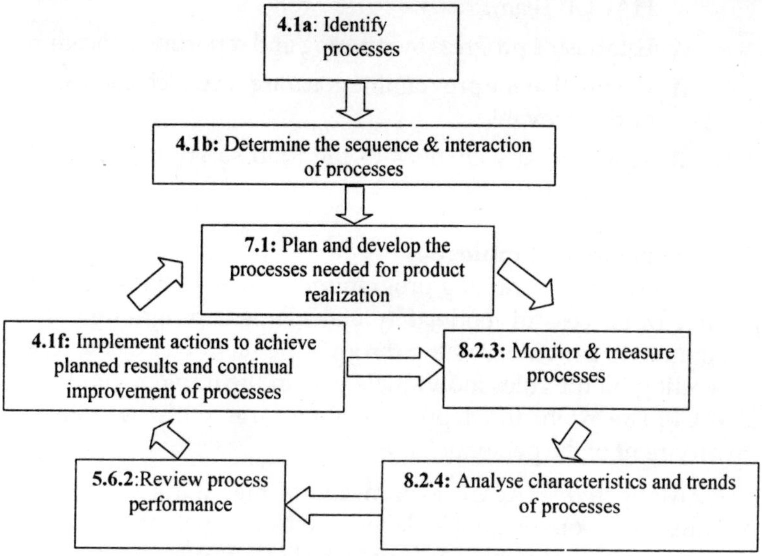

Figure 21.5: An Example of Process Approach

Application of HACCP System

Prerequisites for Implementation of HACCP

Management Commitment

The successful application of HACCP system depends entirely on the top management of the dairy. Therefore it requires commitment and involvement of the top management at different stages of development and implementation of the system. This can come only if there is complete understanding of what HACCP actually is, what benefits it can offer to the industry, what is really involved and what resources will be required. The management should make its intent to quality and safety clear by defining its policy and should be responsible to:

- ✰ Approve and drive food safety management programme,
- ✰ Ensure that the programme continues to move forward and remains valid,

- Appoint a management representative and HACCP team,
- Ensure that adequate resources are made available to the HACCP Team,
- Establish a progress monitoring and reporting procedure,
- Ensure that the programme goals are set which are realistic and achievable,
- Approve any changes to the food safety management programme.

Empowerment of Employees

The awareness training programme is an essential step in the journey of successful food safety management programme. It is imperative to provide training through the hierarchy of the dairy depending on the roles individuals play in the implementation of HACCP. The extent and depth of training varies with the degree of involvement of the personnel.

An effective HACCP as a means of managing food safety requires the people responsible for it to be competent. The single most important element in setting up a HACCP System is training. Training not only provides the technical skills required in implementing HACCP but also helps in changing attitudes of people to appreciate the importance of food safety.

Facility Specific Requirements

In addition to management commitment and employee empowerment, the dairy must have following in place to meet International Code of Practice for General Principle of Food Hygiene enunciated by Codex Alimentarius Commission:

1. Design and Facilities
2. Personal hygiene
3. Supplier control
4. Specifications
5. Machinery and equipment maintenance
6. Cleaning and sanitation
7. Chemical control
8. Receiving storage and shipping
9. Product recall programme

10. Pest control programme
11. Calibration of measuring devices
12. Compliance to food laws

It essential for the implementation of HACCP programme to comply with the national food laws. Therefore for food industries in India it required that they should identify applicable provision of the Prevention of Food Adulteration Act and Rules.

Preliminary Steps

Step 01: Establishment of a Multi-disciplinary Team

Development of HACCP based food safety management programme requires a multi-disciplinary team with appropriate expertise in veterinary health, production, microbiology, toxicology, public health, food technology, health, chemistry and engineering according to the nature of study. This cross-functional expertise is necessary to analyze all physical, chemical, and biological hazards. If the people drawn in the team are not specialists and are not properly trained andexperienced, HACCP System is unlikely to be effective.

Step 02: Describe the Product

The dairy product(s) description should include the major raw material, food ingredients, preservation and packing materials used

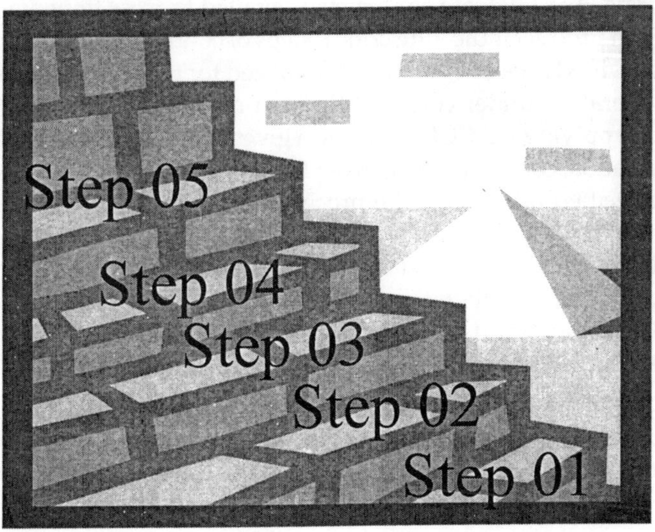

and their impact on food safety. This can also include a brief description of how the process occurs and/products are produced and stored. It would be useful if hazards that may exist either in ingredients or in packing material are identified. A description of the method of distribution includes type of transport and any special consideration to maintain product safety. For example Ice cream is described as a frozen ready to eat product containing both pasteurized and unpasteurized components. The skim milk powder, butter, sugar and water are pasteurized while the flavourings, nuts and chocolate are added without further heat processing. Air is also whipped into the product at freezing.

Step 03: Identify Intended Use

The intended use should be based on the expected uses of the product by the end user or consumer. It should be indicated how the product is to be used including if it is to be fully cooked before consumption, what preparations will be needed, what will be serving requirements, shelf life etc. If consumer has special consideration such as infant or geriatrics it should be made clear so that necessary emphasis may be given to safeguard their special interest. For instance ice cream is consumed without further processing by general population including high risk groups but infant milk food is meant for infants and is given special consideration.

Step 04: Construct a Process Flow Diagram

The HACCP team constructs a detailed Process flow diagram for each product indicating critical steps of control. Each step within the specified area of operation is analyzed for the particular part of the operation under consideration to produce the flow diagram. When applying HACCP system to a given operation, consideration is operation, consideration is given to steps preceding and following the specified operation. The process flow diagram is used as the basis of the hazard analysis and should therefore contain sufficient technical detail for the study to progress. Each step within the specified area of operation should be analyzedarea of operation should be analyzed for the particular part of the operation under consideration to produce the flow diagram (Figure 21.6).

The process flow diagram is verified by the HACCP team at site to confirm the processing operation against the flow diagram during all stages and hours of operation and amend the flow diagram where

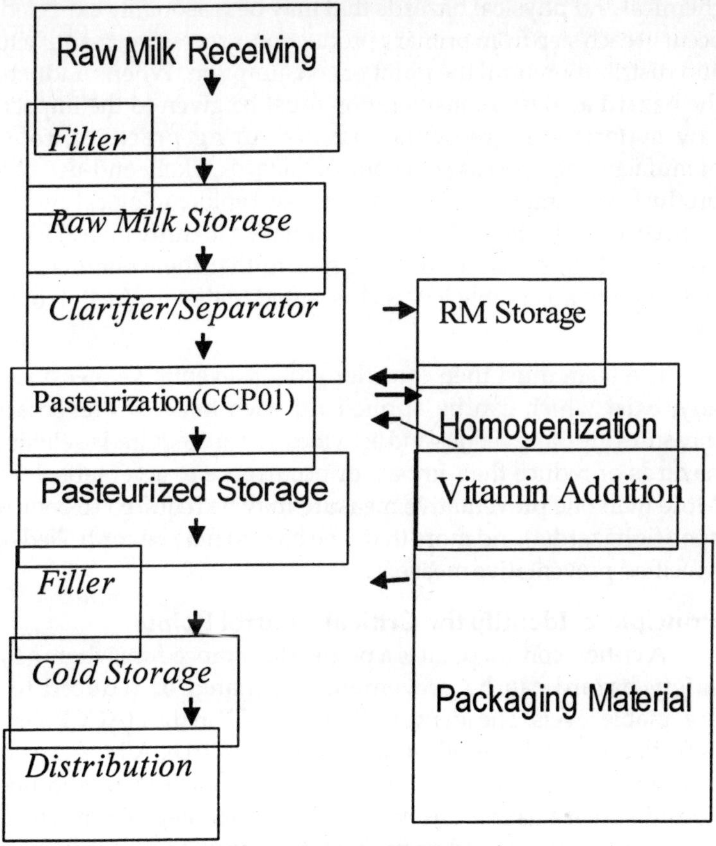

Figure 21.6: A Model Flow Diagram

appropriate.This is partly in-office exercise and partly on-site activity. In -office exercise includes dissecting the process stage and discussing the implications of process parameters and then they verified at the site.The verification of the flow diagram at site is done by actually walking through the dairy to check the accuracy and completeness and make sure that the steps listed on the diagram describe what really occurs in producing the product.

Primary Steps Based on HACCP Principles

Principle 1: Conduct Hazard Analysis

When the process flow diagram is completed and verified, the HACCP team conducts a hazard analysis and lists all the biological, chemical and physical hazards that may be reasonably expected to occur at each step from primary production, processing, manufacture and distribution until the point of consumption. When conducting the hazard analysis, consideration must be given to the impact of raw materials, ingredients, manufacturing practices, role of manufacturing processes to control hazards, likely end-use of the product, consumer populations at risk and epidemological evidence relative to food safety. The team should then identify in the HACCP plan which hazards are of such nature that their elimination or reduction to acceptable levels is essential to the production of safe food.

The team must then consider what preventative measures, if any, exist which can be applied for each hazard. Preventative measures are those actions and activities that are required to eliminate hazards or reduce their impact or occurrence to acceptable levels. More than one preventative measure may be required to control a specific hazard(s) and more than one hazard may be controlled by a specified preventative measure.

Principle 2: Identify the Critical Control Points

A critical control point is a point/step/procedure where a food safety hazard can be prevented, eliminated or reduced to an acceptable levels. The identification of a CCP in the HACCP system is facilitated by the application of a decision tree. All hazards that may be reasonably expected to occur, at each step, should be considered. If a hazard has been identified at a step where control is necessary for safety, and no preventative measure exists at that step, or any other, then the product or process should be modified at that step, or at any earlier or later stage, to include a preventative measure. Application of the decision tree determines whether the step is a CCP for the identified hazard.

Principle 3: Establish Critical Limits for Each CCP

Since the critical control points define the boundaries between safe and unsafe products, it is vital that they are specified at the correct levels and validated at each criteria. The HACCP team should therefore fully understand the criteria governing safety at each CCP in order to set the appropriate critical limits. Critical limits must be specified for each preventative measure. In some cases more than one critical limit will be elaborated at a particular step. Criteria often used include measurements of temperature, time, moisture level, pH, and available chlorine, and sensory parameters such as visual appearance and texture.

Principle 4: Establish a Monitoring System for Each CCP

Monitoring is one of the most important aspects of the HACCP system. It is the scheduled measurement a CCP relative to its critical limits. The monitoring procedures must be able to detect loss of control at the CCP and provide information in time for corrective action to regain control of the process. The frequency of monitoring must be sufficient to ensure that the CCP is under control. Most monitoring procedures for CCPs will need to be done rapidly because they relate to on-line processes and there will not be time for lengthy analytical testing. Physical and chemical measurements are often preferred to microbiological testing because they may be done rapidly and can often indicate the microbiological control of the product. All records and documents associated with monitoring CCPs must be signed by the person(s) doing the monitoring and by a responsible reviewing official(s) of the company.

Principle 5: Establish Corrective Actions

Specific corrective actions must be developed for each CCP in the HACCP system in order to deal with deviations when they occur.The actions must ensure that the CCP has been brought under control. Actions taken must also include proper disposition of the nonconforming product. Deviation and product disposition procedures must be documented in the HACCP record keeping. Corrective action should also occur when monitoring results indicate a trend towards loss of control at a CCP. Action should be taken to bring the process back into control before the deviation leads to a safety hazard.

Principle 6: Establish Verification Procedures

The HACCP system should include verification procedures to provide assurance that HACCP system is being complied with on day-today basis. This can be done most effectively by using audit method. Monitoring and auditing methods, procedures and tests,including random sampling and analysis, can be used to determine if the HACCP system is working correctly. The frequency of verification should be sufficient to confirm that the HACCP system is working effectively. Examples of verification activities include:

1. Review of the HACCP system and its records.
2. Review of deviations and product dispositions.
3. Confirmation if CCPs are under control.
4. Validation of established critical limits.

Principle 7: Establish Record Keeping and Documentation

Efficient and accurate record keeping is essential to the application of a HACCP system. Records need to be kept of all areas which are critical to product safety to demonstrate that the HACCP system is in compliance with the documented system. Documentation of HACCP procedures at all steps should be

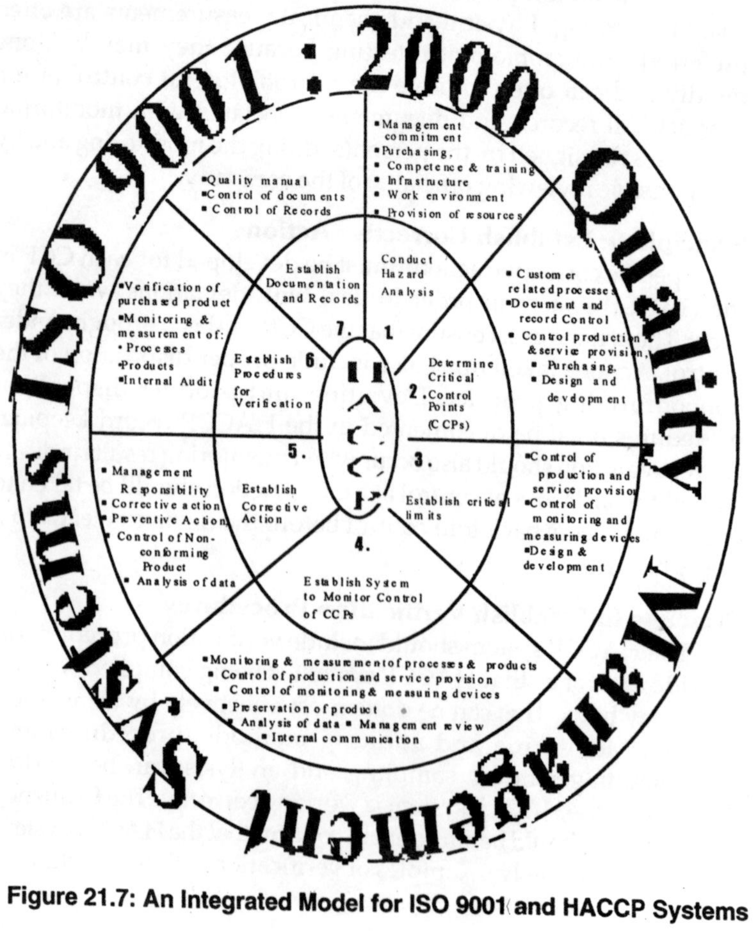

Figure 21.7: An Integrated Model for ISO 9001 and HACCP Systems

included and assembled in a manual.Records are useful in providing a basis for analysis of trends as well as for internal investigation of any food safety incidents which may occur.

Synergizing ISO 9000 and HACCP

Both these management systems - one design to build quality and another to build safety are compatible with each other and synergising them will provide strength to both. The seven principles of HACCP are the building block for food safety management system and eight principles implemented through five elements of ISO 9001 are the building block for Quality management system.

The two systems are closely related and are compatible with each other (Figure 21.7). Twinning the two systems will give synergetic effect for better results.Therefore, the best way is to use ISO 9000 route to manage HACCP to ensure quality and safety of food. Both the systems are quality assurance systems, designed to provide maximum confidence that a specified acceptable level of quality and safety are being achieved at an economic cost.

Chapter 22

Sensory Quality Evaluation of Milk and Milk Products and their Safety Standards

Sunita Mishra,
Department of Home Science, (Food and Nutrition), M.M.V., B.H.U., Varanasi

Milk is one of the most essential of all foods because milk is one of the most completes single foods available in nature for health and promotion of growth. In provides nourishment for the young as well as other age groups. The principal sources of milk for human consumption are cow, buffalo, goat, sheep, camel etc.

Milk is composed of milk fat, milk protein, milk sugar, milk ash and salts and vitamins.

Nutritional Products of Milk

The common milk products are:

Unfermented Products

1. *Skimmed Milk-* Skimmed milk and milk powder is made by the roller process and the dried powder is removed by scrapping.
2. *Toned Milk-* is a useful source of proteins for malnourished children, pregnancy, school going children, hospital

sports and other public institution. Double Toned milk contain only 1.5 per cent fat.

3. Milk cream-Milk fat is known as cream, which floats on the surface of the milk.
4. Malai-Malai is known as clotted cream. After milk is boiled and allowed to cool, a thick layer of fat and coagulated proteins collects at the surface. Malai supplies 3.5 per cent of proteins, 30 per cent of fat, and 300 Kcal/per 100 gm of malai.
5. Khoa-Khoa is milk in which the water content is reduced to 20 per cent and 25 per cent khoa supplies 24 per cent of protein 41 per cent of fat, 28 per cent of carbohydrate, 580 kcal/per tablespoon.
6. Chana (Cottage Cheese) Chana is prepared by adding lemon juice to boiling milk or by acetic acid, this precipitates casein. The liquid part (whey) is strained through a cloth and chhane is collected. It supplies 15 per cent of protein, 22 per cent of fat, 5 per cent carbohydrate and 280 kcal/ per 100 gm of channa.

Fermented Products

Dahi (Curd)

Dahi is known as curd, when milk is boiled and bacteria present in the milk are killed, then the milk is cooled at 37°C the "starter" is added (which is generally the residual Dahi from the previous preparation, rich in lactic acid organisms). Dahi has the same calorie value as the milk.

Ghee

Ghee is a fermented product. A kind of butter is produced from Dahi (Curd) which i s boiled to evaporate the moisture. The composition of cow and buffalo ghee is similar is contains 99 per cent fat, mostly saturated 3800 I.U. (Internation Unit) Vit A/per 100 gm of ghee. Ghee contain cholesterol oxide.

Cheese

In India cottage cheese (Chana) is an unfermented milk product, where in the west it is a fermented product. There are over 400, varieties of cheese. Cheese contains casein, vitamin 'A', calcium phosphorus, thiamine and riboflavin.

Nutritional Importance of Milk

Milk is considered to be one of the balance food to meet the needs of human nutrition. It is rich is high quality protein, carbohydrate, calcium, phosphorous riboflavin and other B vitamins. Milk is poor as a source of vitamin D, vitamin C and Iron milk proteins are one of the highest quality proteins and equal the meat proteins in nutritions efficiency. Milk protein are rich in lysine. Milk is used in the treatment of diseases like peptic ulcer, protein deficiency, acute illness and convalescence, increasing weight, soya milk for (weight loss)

Sensory Evolution

Sensory quality evaluation of any food product, depends on nutritional and other hidden attributes, and sensory quality is assessed by means of human sensory organs. Qualities of foods are evaluated by sense organs-eye, nose and mouth or by use of instrument.

Sensory evaluation consists of judging the quality of food by a panel of judges. The evaluation deals which measuring, analyzing and interpreting the qualities of food as they are perceived by the sense of sight, taste, touch and hearing.

Sensory evaluation may be designed to reflect common preference, to maintain the quality of food at a given standard, for the assessment of procen variation, cost reduction, product improvement, new market development and market analysis.

Selection of Panel of Judges

An unbiased individual would suffice for tasting of any product. However human judgment is not always consistent, physical condition of the individual, psychological factors and environmental factors may affects ones judgment. Further, one individual may not be able to discriminate different aspects of the food, quality, for these reasons, for Sensory evaluation, a panel of judges is used. The number of members in the trained panel should be small, varying from 5 to 10. The semi trained panel should consist of 25 to 30 members.

Preparation of Samples

Careful sampling of the food is necessary for sensory evaluation. A well mixed homogeneous sample should be taken. Samples should be takes from the same area. Samples to be tested should be prepared by identical methods. All samples in a series should be at the same temperature.

Types of Test

Different sensory test are employed for food evaluation. The test are grouped into 4 types : they are difference test, rating test, sensitivity tests and descriptive tests.

Difference Test

Difference test are used to determine, it these is any difference between or among samples. The three basic types of difference tested are simple difference, Quantitative difference and Quality preference difference. The methods of difference testing Commonly used are the paired comparison, due trio and triangle test.

In paired Comparison test two samples one standard and the other experimental, are presented to the panelists to determine, if the samples are different.

The due trio test employees three samples two identical and one different. The panelists are first given the reference sample and then the other two samples are given successively in random order and asked to match one of them with the first.

The triangle test also employs three samples, two identical and one different. All the three samples are presented simultaneously to the panelists who are asked to determine to determine which of the three is the old sample.

Rating Tests

In a ranking test, judges are asked to rank a series of samples in the increasing or decreasing order, such as flavour, odour, colour texture. Rating test are defined by scales or score. A hedonic rating test is used to measure the degree of pleasurable and unpleasurable experience of the food product on a scale of 9 points from "like extremely to dislike extremely". The numerical scoring test is used to evaluate a particular characteristic of one of more samples indicating the rating as excellent, good, fair and poor.

Sensitivity Threshold Test

This test measure the ability of the individual to smell, taste, feel specific characteristics in food or beverages.

Descriptive Tests

These tests help identify the perceptual characteristics of a product and expren them on a scale. The test include flavour profile tests test to describe the structure and inner make up of foods.

Judging

The environment is an important factor in judging food. There should notbe any distraction so that the judges can concentrate. The best time of the day for Sensory testing is an hour after any normal meal *i.e.* mid-morning or mid afternoon. The panel members should not smoke, chew pan or supari or take intoxicant for at least half an hour before the test. Use of odoriferous substances should be avoided.

Results

The result of evaluation are recorded in cards, for different type methods. The data are tabulated, averaged and analyzed for the answer, to the question posed in the experiment.

Food Safety and Security

Food safety issues have been the most wanted intervention in the field of nutrition all over the world. The importance of optimal nutrition for health and human development is well recognised. Though there has been a remarkable improvement in the quality and quantity of food consumed, food safety issues have an increasing profile on a global basis. India, a fast growing developing country, also faces the food safety problems. However food safety education for food handlers. Consumer awareness and intrest in food safety matter a lot. There is health problems due to unsanitary handling conditions lack of hygiene, using chemical additives of no nutritional value.

Food Standards

To check malpractices "prevention of food adulteration Act" enacted by the Indian parliament in 1954.

To provide pure and wholesome food to the consumer and to protect them from fraudulent and deceptive trade practices.

The important food standards in India are:

- F.P.O. (Food Product Order)
- "AGMARK" (The Agmark Standard)

☆ ISI (The Indian Standards Institution)

☆ H.A.C.C.P. Hazand Analysis Critical Control

There is a disparity between the urban and rural areas in food development. Under nutrition and over nutrition coexist.

Food Laws and Rugulations

Food laws came into existence for a number of reasons.

1. To maintain the quality of food produced in the country.
2. To prevent exploitation of the consumer by the sellers.
3. To safe guard the health of the consumers.
4. To establish criteria for quality of food products, since more and more foods were eaten in processed, rather than in natural forms.

Where to Register Complaint

The consumers can register their complaints with the consumer forums, which are located in every district, at the state as well as national levels.

Compensation up to 5 lakhs value can be registered at District level consumer forum.

Compensation is between 5-20 lakhs then the complaint is to be registered at the state level forum.

Compensation above 20 lakhs can be registered with the national consumer forum.

Complaints should have:

☆ Full name and address of the complaining person.

☆ Fill name and address of the opponent.

☆ Detailed facts about the complaint.

☆ Documents relating to the claims in the letter vouchers, receipts, bill, card etc.

☆ Monetary compensation or relief claimed by the complaining person.

Discussion and Conclusion

Food safety sustainability is possible through the following consumer's awareness:

While making a purchase for more than Rs. 20/- every consumer should ask for a proper bill for the bill book of the dealer.

While purchasing one should read the label properly quality, weight, quality, price, date of manufacturing etc, should be mentioned duly.

Product which display quality control signs like. FPO "agmark" "ISI" and others' should be given priority while purchasing various goods.

Consumer should not purchase goods only on the basis of advertisements purchases should be base on the value of the product.

One should not purchase products from the black market or any unauthorised means. Purchasing through illegal means encourages black marketing.

Consumers can register their complaints to district supply officer in respect of weight and measure, adulteration or against black marketing.

Consumer can approach consumer guidance society or District Supply Officer for obtaining compensation for defaults.

Every consumer should known the functioning of consumer forum.

Recommendations

An action plan was prepared in the city with some notable recommendations like listing of vendors. Food handlers Identification of Hawking area, area wise layout plan, proper cleanness, food safety measure, proper coordination with Varanasi municipal corporation, food Inspectors Police and Government of Uttar Pradesh License to vendors, Shopkeeper, Provision of potable water, Garbage and waste water disposal facilities, Awareness and education to public, vendor, Regular Analysis of food and water sample. Traffic and pedestrian movement etc. were recommended as effective food safety measure.

Chapter 23

Abstract of the Lecture Entitled Milk and its Products in Indian Tradition

V.C. Srivastava

Department of Animal Husbandry and Dairying, Institute of Agricultural Sciences, Banaras Hindu University, Varanasi

1. Dairy-farming or dairying is universal phenomenon and its history goes back to the prehistoric period. As profession/occupation and domestic and commercial industry it continues its development throughout the long history of human kind. Even at present it is one of the most popular scientific industry in developed as well as developing countries.
2. India developed dairy farming along with agriculture right from the Neolithic period in the wake of domestication of catties and plants. Dairy farming continued to flourish in the protohistoric period as there are some evidences in the Harappa Culture. However the details of cattle-breeding, cattle-rearing and cattle-herding and the production and distribution of milk and its products can not be worked out on the basis of material remains of the Harrapa culture.

3. The picture of dairy-farming becomes somewhat clearer for the Vedic period. The present lecture is limited to a survey of Milk and its products in the Vedic tradition. Cow is one of the two main sources of milk, the other being the she buffalo. The Vedic literature is full of references to cows while buffalo is scarcely mentioned as such the lecture will dwell upon cow's milk and its products in the Vedic literature.
4. The terms–*Go* has been so profusely used in the Vedic literature that one schools of historians has theorized that the early Vedic people were nomadic pasforalist. But this view has not been accepted by another school of historians who believe that the occupations of dairy-man along with pastoralism, forest-dwelling, agriculture, trade and crafts flourished side by side from the early Vedic times onwards. The Vedic index refers to cattle-hoarding and dairying along with agriculture, trade and craftsmanship, which found significant part of socio-economic milieu of early Vedic times and later.
5. The Rigveda has full hymn (VI, 28) dedicated to cow. Cow has been venerated as a deity and symbol of wealth. Cow's milk is mixed in the Soma drink for strength. The Rigveda prays for abundant cows who give profuse milk are easily milked and have many calves. There are references to cow-pen (Goshtha). They have been identified with India- the highest God of me Aryans. Full care was takes for provision of healthy grass and pure water. Care was also taken so that thieves and evil persons may not be able to possess them. The main products–milk, butter, ghee and curd formed the main items of food- Milk, butter and ghee were symbols of fertility. These items were used in sacrifices and rituals.
6. Cows had been so important in the Vedic society that a rishi like Visvamitra stole cow kamdhenu of Vasistha. In later Vedic literature also cows and their products have been extolled. The Atharvaveda has full hymn in praise of cows. The Yajurveda prays for cows milking with ease and yielding abundant milk and ghee. The Brahmaas, the Upanisads and the Sutras have exalted cows.

7. Cows were milked thrice a day in the Upanisads. There are many rituals for the welfare of the catties in the sutras. The later Vedic literature is full of references to milk and milk products specially butter and ghee as source of food as well as sacrifice.
8. The cows were treated for various diseases including infertility. The process of making curd is also mentioned. The varieties and types of cows have also been mentioned.
9. Dairy-farming was an integral part of the unified concept of life in Vedic times. It was in harmony with nature-sentient and insentient. This view was based on the Vedic belief that every creature is a part of divinity.

Chapter 24

Sweets from Heat and Acid-Coagulated Milk Products

Jai Singh

Deoartment of Animal Husbanry and Dairying, BHU, Varanasi

Majority of the people in India are Vegetarian. They are preparing their diet with the addition of milk as it is easily available where lactating animals are maintained. Milk and milk products are the only cheaper source of nutritional food which is more helpful for balancing the diet for our population, particularly for vegetarians who have not much option to take their food other than milk, as a source of animal proteins. The requirement of animal protein is about 20 per cent of total protein in the diet.

Till to day, we don't have minimum facilities at every corner of the country to save milk quality for desired period. Therefore, it is been deemed essential to continue on the preparation of milk products in our prevailing conditions. Milk products are the concentrated form of nutrients, palatable, durable and easy to transport. Khoa is one of the best examples for it. With the addition of sugar this product is made more palatable which can be kept for longer duration. The Khoa based indigenous sweets are mainly Peda, Burfi and Kalakand.

Instead of Kalakand, Srikhand is also an acid coagulated milk sweet. Srikhand is a Dahi based products prepared with the addition of sugar, but it is not so popular in the country.

The Kalakand is gaining more popularity in modern societies of the developing countries of the world. This is prepare with heat and acid coagulated whole milk alongwith sugar. In place of whole milk, skim milk or separated milk can also be used but the products will not be of desired quality.

Classification of Indian Sweets

1. Form of Solids
   - (*i*) Khoa based
     - (*a*) Sweet Khoa – Peda, Barfi, Gulabjamun etc.
     - (*b*) Acid coagulated – Kalakand
   - (*ii*) Chhana based – Sandesh, Rasgolla etc.
   - (*iii*) Khoa and Chhana both- Pantooa
   - (*iv*) Ghee residue – Chocolate
2. Semi Solids – Srikhand
3. Liquid form – Kheer

Total Solids Present in Different Species of Milk

Higher total solids in the milk is an indication of higher recovery in dried product. The T.S. in some of the milk are given in Table 24.1.

Table 24.1: Total Solids in Different Species of Milk

Species	*Percentage*
Boffalo	18.26
Ewe	16.43
Cow (Desi)	14.72
Camel	13.79
Goats	12.86
Cow milk (Exotic)	12.68

Casein NCN (non casein nitrogen) in Cow milk – 80 : 20

Human milk – 40:60

Ingredients Required for Kalakand Preparation

The different ingredients are given in Table 24.2.

Table 24.2: Ingredients Required for Different Type of Kalakand

	Type of Kalaland		
Ingredients	*Simple*	*Special*	*Creamkand (Simple or Special)*
Milk	1.0 Litre	1.0 Litre	1.0 Litre
Sugar	60 gm	60 gm	60 gm
Citric acid	0.5 gm	0.5 gm	.0.5 gm
Silver paper	1 leaf	1 leaf	1 leaf
Pista	—-	A few pieces	May or may not be
Cardamom	—-	A few sticks	May or May not be
Sweet dense cream	—-	—-	50 gm

Method of Kalakand Preparation

Take desired quantity of milk in a karahi (properly cleaned) and transfer it over non-smoky intense fire. During heating continuous stearing of milk in a circular manner is required. After 5 minutes of boiling add required quantity of diluted citric acid (1part acid and 5 to 10 parts water) in the milk. At this stage, milk is coagulated which requires vigorous steering to obtain a good quality product. When milk reduced to semi-solids stage add desired quantity of sugar and reduce the intensity of heat immediately. After 5 minutes, when sugar is properly mixed the pista and cardamom can be added. If added, these should be mixed properly into the whole content. The karahi is removed from the fire. The finished products is set in a greasy tray or plate and allow to cool at room temperature. If desired, this can be decorated with sliced pista and silver paper. Cut into pieces of desire size and shape to serve.

Steps for Kalakand Production

Sweet Whole Milk

↓

Filtration of Milk

↓

Standardization of milk

↓ (Desirable fat 5 per cent and SNF 9.5 per cent)

Heating of milk (On boiling temperature)

↓ 5 Minutes

Addition of Citric acid (1 Ml. in 10 ml. water for 1 lt. milk)

↓ (Vigorous stirring)

Dough stage

↓

Addition of sugar (6 per cent of milk)

↓ Reduced heat and stirring

Addition of cardamom and Pista

↓

Setting of mixed (in greasy tray)

↓

Cutting and Shaping

↓ ⟶ Dressing by cream ↓

Packaging of Kalakand

↓

Storage and Transport

Dressing by Cream

For the preparation of creamkand a thin layer of sweet and fresh cream is prepared on the upper portion of the product before its decoration. Smear of cream may only be prepared when the product become cool.

Yield of Kalakand

The recovery of Kalakand is higher to khoa due to mixing of sugar.

Defects in Kalakand

Flavour

1. *Smoky*: Due to smoky fire and burned of product.
2. *Rensid*: Hydrolysis due to lipase action during storage.

Body and Texture

1. *Hard body:* Excessive low fat, low moisture and starch adulteration in milk.
2. *Coarse texture:* Low fat, low moisture, high temperature and lower rate of stirring.

Colour and Appearance

1. *Dry surface:* Low fat content.
2. *Browning:* Excessive high heat, low speed of stirring
3. *Mouldy surface:* High humidity of storage room, leak of packaging.

Score Card of Kalakand

Table 24.3: Score Card in Kalakand

Item	*Perfect Score*
Flavour	45
Body and Texture	35
Colour and Appearance	15
Package	05
Total	100

- ☆ Score card more than 90: Very good Kalakand
- ☆ Score card 80-89: Good Kalakand
- ☆ Score card 70-79: poor Kalakand
- ☆ Score card less than 70: Bad Kalakand

Packaging of Kalakand

Kalakand is packaged with waxy paper in container or box to save its quality for longer duration.

Storage

It can be stored for 5 to 7 days at room temperature and approximately for 14 days at normal refrigeration temperature.

Kalakand

It is acidic, lacerable on knuckle, adaptable, desiccated delicious products which bears kerf, acquit, native-nectarous characters in the product.

K: Knuckle (To press with fingers)

A: Acidic

L: Lacerable (easily brokable)

A: Adaptable

K: Kerf (Groove or channel made by cutting with saw)

A: Acquit (To set free on applying light pressure)

N: Native –Nectarous

D: Desiccated- delicious

Chapter 25

Technology of Manufacture of Rabri

K.P. Singh

Reader,

Department of Animal Husbandry and Dairying

R.B.S. College, Bichpuri, Agra, U.P.

Introduction

The term 'Indian Dairy Products' refers to those milk products which originated in undivided India. The importance of milk and milk products in this country has been recognised since Vedic times (five thousand years ago), and the variety of ways in which milk is used for the preparation of indigenous products has been developed more or less as an art. However, only recently, these methods have been studied in detail on scientific lines.

Until the year 1940, there was very little published information on the preparation of these products. The credit for the first publication on the subject goes to Dr. W.L. Davies, the first Director of Dairy Research, Indian Dairy Research Institute, Bangalore (now, National Dairy Research Institute). Within a span of three or four decades since Dr. 'Davies' book appeared, considerable research has been conducted at the National Dairy Research Institute and other places on indigenous dairy products (Sukumar, De, 1980).

The milk and milk products offer an equally perfect medium for the growth of several micro organisms which thrive one the sugar (lactose), fat and/or proteins of milk. The multiplication of these organisms leads first to the smell and taste of acidity, and soon after to the clotting and curdling of milk. The aim has always been, therefore, to conserve either all or as many as possible of the constituents of milk in the form most akin to that in the original milk (Rangappa and Achaya, 1974).

Concentration and partial desiccation of milk and the addition of preservatives like sugar and fillers like flour to resulting concentrates have given rise to various unfermented milk products. While some of these are peculiar to India, many have their counterparts among the whole milk products.

Comparison with Western Dairy Products

Broadly speaking, Indian dairy products, with the exception of ghee, have lower keeping quality than western dairy products. Further, Indian products are invariably prepared on a small scale, while the reverse is true of western products. The various Indian dairy products and their corresponding western counter parts have been presented as under.

Table 25.1: Indian Dairy Products and their Western Counter Parts

Indian Dairy Products		*Corresponding Western Products*
A. Concentrated whole milk products		
1.	Kheer/Basandi	Condensed milk
2.	Khoa/Mawa	Evaporated milk
3.	Rabri	Clotted cream
4.	Kulfi	Ice-cream
B. Coagulated milk products		
1.	Dahi	Curd/Yoghurt
2.	Srikhand	Curd (sweetened)
3.	Paneer	Soft cheese
4.	Chhana	Lactic coagulated green cheese
C. Products of the clarified butter fat industry		
1.	Makkhan	Butter
2.	Ghee*	Butter oil
3.	Lassi	Butter milk
4.	Ghee Residue**	–

*: Samna (or Masli) in Egyptian; **: Mourta in Egyptian.

The western and northern regions of the country consume a major amount of milk in direct or indirect liquid form. On the other hand, milk consumption in the southern and eastern region is largely through tea and coffee. Out of the total production of milk, 46 per cent is consumed as fluid milk and 7 per cent as curd. Details of the different forms of milk consumption are laid down as under.

Table 25.2: Different Forms of Milk Consumption

Products	*Consumption in Terms of per cent*
Whole milk	46
Ghee	28
Curd	7
Butter	6.58
Khoa	5.5
Milk Powder	3.8
Cheese	2.0
Others	1.12

Source: Indian Statistical Institute, 1997.

Technological Studies on Rabri

Among indigenous milk products of India, rabri is an important indigenous milk product quite popular in northern and eastern part of India. This is an especially prepared concentrated and sweetened whole milk product, containing several layers of clotted cream. While the milk is slowly evaporated (without being stirred) at simmering temperature in a Karahi over an open fire, pieces of skin which form on the surface of the milk are continuously broken up and moved to the cooler parts of the Karahi. When the volume of milk has been reduced to about one eighth of the original volume, sugar is added to it; then layers of clotted cream are immersed in the mixture and the finished product is obtained by heating whole mass for another short period.

Flow Digram of Method of Manufacture of Rabri

Receiving milk

↓

Filtration

↓

Testing of milk and Standardization
(5 per cent fat and 8.5 per cent SNF)*

↓

Heating milk in open Karahi at Simmering Temp.

↓

Moving of cream layer on cooler part of Karahi

↓

Addition of sugar

↓

Mixing of layer of clotted cream

↓

Heating mass for short period

↓

Used/sold for direct consumption

Selection of Milk

In the manufacture of rabri, the fresh milk with pleasant flavour should be used.

Filtration

To remove any type of visible dirt, dust, or fodder particles the milk is filtered through double layered muslin cloth.

Testing and Standardization of Milk

To obtain the product of uniform and best acceptable quality the received milk is tested for fat and SNF conent and standardized to 5 per cent fat and 8.5 per cent SNF(Singh and Gupta, 1989).

Heating of Milk

The standardized milk is transferred in a shallow karahi and allowed to heat at simmering temperature over the open fire.

Moving of Cream Layer

During heating at simmering temperature the layer of clotted cream are lifted with the help of splint and transferred on cooler part of the karahi.

Addition of Sugar

When the volume of milk in karahi has been reduced to one eighth of the original volume, the sugar (previously dried) at the rate of 5 per cent of total volume of milk is added to the liquid residue and mixed.

Mixing of Clotted Cream

The layers of cream (in the form of pieces) are scraped from the cooler part of karahi and immersed in the liquid residue.

Heating of Mass

The mass of clotted cream is heated in the karahi for short period for proper mixing of liquid residue with flakes of clotted cream.

The prepared product is used or sold for direct consumption.

Food and Nutritive Value

As rabri contains all the constituents (milk solids) in an approximately five fold concentration, with added sugar, its food and nutritive value are very high.

Table 25.3: Chemical Composition of Rabri (Percentage) (Rangappa and Achaya, 1974)

Moisture	*Fat*	*Protein*	*Lactose*	*Ash*	*Sugar*
30.00	20.00	10.00	17.00	3.00	20.00

An experiment to "*Standardize the technique for the preparation of rabri and input-output relations*" was conducted by (Singh and Gupta, 1989). Rabri prepared from milk standardised to different levels of fat and SNF and with various concentrations of added sugar in each combination (Table 25.1). The temperature recorded at different stages during preparation of rabri from three combinations of milk having different levels of fat/SNF and sugar was almost the same. The temperature differed only slightly with a tendency to rise up with increasing concentration of cane sugar, but, these were no substaintial. The overall mean temperatures (irrespective of sugar concentration) were almost same for the three combinations of milk used in the preparation of product. The observations further revealed that there was a steady increase in the temperature as the volume of milk diminished due to removal of successive layers of skin from the surface of milk. The highest temperature recorded at the end of the process was approximately 209°F. The skin formation time was decidedly influenced by the intensity of temperature and fat/SNF levels. Higher temperature caused quick skin formation. The skin formation time at higher temperature was lowest in combination C and highest in combination A at all the levels of added sugar. However, the total time required for rabri making from 2 kg milk did not differ substantially in different combinations of milk used for rabri making.

The product (rabri) prepared from each combination of fat and SNF using different levels of added sugar was subjected to sensory evaluation by a panel of 5 judges constituted from members of staff of the Department who were well versed with the process to sensory evaluation. On the basis of sensory evaluation, the following combinations of fat, SNF and sugar were found to give a product of good/excellent quality (Table 25.4).

- ☆ Combination A- 4 per cent fat, 8.5 per cent SNF and 25 per cent sugar
- ☆ Combination B- 5 per cent fat, 8.5 per cent SNF and 25 per cent sugar
- ☆ Combination C- 6 per cent fat, 9 per cent SNF and 25 per cent sugar

Out of all the combinations, combination B was found to be the best in respect of all sensory attributes.

Chemical Quality of Rabri

The samples of rabri collected from markets had higher acidity than control samples, because the samples were prepared from stall milk. The control sample prepared from fresh milk had lower acidity. Control A and B samples had slightly higher, T.S., fat, lactose and sugar than market samples. The overall markets and overall control samples had almost same chemical make up except the acidity of the product.

Input-output relati^n for each combination yielding an acceptable quality (good/excellent) of product was worked out from the economic point of view. The degree of concentration of milk constituents into the product was also ascertained.

The yield of the product was highest in combination C against almost same input (milk, sugar, fuel, labour etc.) used in all the

Table 25.4: Sensory Score of Rabri

Sl.No.	Type of Samples	No. of Samples	Appearance (20 Marks)	Flavour (45 Marks)	Body Texture (35 Marks)	Total Score (100 Marks)
1.	Agra	20	16.650 ± 0.302	35.950 ± 0.724	28.900 ± 0.416	81.500 ± 1.144
2.	Mathura	20	15.700 ± 0.325	36.950 ± 0.651	26.700 ± 0.448	79.350 ± 1.164
3.	Control A	5	17.800 ± 0.374	42.800 ± 0.374	32.600 ± 0.748	93.200 ± 1.068
4.	Control B	7	18.714 ± 0.840	43.286 ± 0.286	33.857 ± 0.143	95.857 ± 0.459
5.	Control C	7	18.000 ± 0.309	42.143 ± 0.459	32.429 ± 0.429	92.571 ± 0.685
	Overall markets		16.175 ± 0.232	36.450 ± 0.487	27.800 ± 0.349	80.425 ± 0.823
	Overall control		18.211 ± 0.181	42.737 ± 0.240	33.000 ± 0.286	93.947 ± 0.521

combinations (Table 25.2). Yield of the product was lowest in combination A, possibly because of lower per cent of fat and SNF in milk. Combination B gave a higher yield (output) than combination A, because the former contained a higher per cent of fat in milk.

Since, the output (yield) was highest in combination C, it gave the maximum profit. Minimum profit was realisable in combination A, where the product yield was lowest and its cost of production more. Combination B gave an intermediate value of both in terms of input and output. The per cent profit was highest in combination C. The per cent profit obtained from rabri making was 28.00, 36.21 and 53.01 from combination A, B and C, respectively. The overall mean profit was 39.07 per cent which indicated that preparation of rabri is a profitable proposition from economic stand point. Commercialization of manufacture of this product on a large scale would bring greater economic returns besides providing a product with uniform quality.

The ratio of concentration of milk constituents was almost same in combination A and B, but it was lower in combination C, possibly because of higher fat and SNF in the milk used in combination C (Table 25.3). It appeared that with increasing contents of fat and SNF, their concentration in the product diminished. In combination A and B, the level of SNF was the same in milk but the fat content was higher in latter. This caused a slightly lower concentration of fat in combination B (4.02) than in combination A (4.17). Since the fat and SNF contents of milk in combination C was the highest, the ratio of concentration of these constituents in this group was the lowest.

The overall mean values indicated that irrespective of combination of milk used in preparation of rabri, the ratio of concentration of fat and SNF was approximately 4 and 6 and 4 and 3.5 with and without added sugar, respectively. The degree of concentration of total solids was 5.30 with added sugar and 3.60 without it.

Conclusion

Trials made to evolve a suitable technology to prepare the product of a uniform quality by employing suitable combinations of Fat/SNF, time temperature relations, concentration of sugar etc. using both cow and buffalo milk and mixture thereof elicited that the milk containing 5 per cent fat, 8.5 per cent SNF and added cane sugar (25 per cent of the finished product) yielded excellent quality product. Input-output relations were also worked out, which suggested that Rabri making is a profitable proposition and if commercialised on a large scale, wc .d bring greater economic returns. The degree of concentration of milk constituents into the product was also ascertained.

References

Davies, W.L. (1958). Indian Indigenous milk products. Pub. By Thacker Spink and Co. Pvt. Ltd., Calcutta.

De, S. (1980). Outlines of dairy technology. *Oxford Univ. Press.* Bombay.

Rangappa, K.S. and Achaya, K.T. (1974). The chemistry and manusfacture of Indian Dairy products. The Bangalore Printing and Pub. Co. Mysore Raod, Banglore City.

Singh, K.P. and Gupta, M.P. (1989). Standardization of technique for the preparation rabri and input-output relations. *Journal of Agriculture and Scientific Research.* **31**: 28-32.

Chapter 26

Soy Food Program in India: Past Present and Future

R.K. Pandey
BHU, Varanasi

Past

In India soybean has been introduced almost four centuries ago and later tried several times. But it was only in mid 20th century however in the hills of Uttar Pradesh and northeast India people have been consuming soybean for centuries.

TVP

Soybean has been in the Indian market for over 30 years but there was not much growth in the market. Except for TVP and use of soy in social programs. A Christian missionary first developed TVP in India in early 70's and later some food and soy processors adopted this technology and started marketing the product. Unfortunately this product could never reach to its full potential and was mainly used as a cheap alternate to vegetables especially in the off seasons. In spite of being the most popular soy product, till recently it was stagnant at about 40-50 TMT. In the last three years there is considerable growth in this product and almost the market doubled. However there is not much development in the product.

Wheat Soy Flour

In India almost for the last thirty years people, especially in north India, have the habit of grinding soybean along with wheat at the local wheat mills to make traditional unleavened flat bread. When ASA was operating in India from Singapore the local consultant in 1996 was successful in convincing the Indian government in approving addition of soy flour to wheat flour to improve protein content. From 1999 ASA started working on commercial promotion of this product. So far there are eight companies who are producing and marketing this product in various Indian markets. In addition to these eight products a number of small-time wheat flour marketers are seeling wheat soy flour as a healthy alternate to whole-wheat flour.

Soymilk and Tofu

In late 80's and early 90's four major food processors started producing soymilk using Japanese technology but unfortunately all the projects failed in 1-2 years of operation. That effected soy consumption heavily. The main reasons for this failure of soymilk were, use of inappropriate technology, wrong positioning of the product and lack of awareness about the goodness of soybean. Not only that non of these processors targeted tofu, which closely resembles traditional Indian milk product *paneer*. Since 1999 ASA started working with small-scale soymilk manufacturers with the help of a part-time consultant and there is considerable increase in this segment, which led to the demand for medium and large scale soymilk units.

Present

TVP

TVP is getting popular in Indian markets very fast. Every year not only a number of new players are coming in to the Indian markets but also all the edible soy processors have started retail marketing of the product. In the current year most of key players started production facilities in south and east India. As of today the total consumption of TVP in India is almost 90 to 95 thousand tons (TMT). TVP was once sold mainly as a bulk commodity has now a number of retail brands with 200 gm packaging.

Wheat Soy Flour

Regarding wheat-soy flour year 2002 has been a good year as one of the U.S. based multination corporation, Agro Tech Foods, started production and marketing of this product in the Indian markets. A number of local wheat flour marketers have also started marketing of this product in the local markets. Most of the edible soy processors and some TVP manufacturers started marketing of defatted soy flour in the different markets where people have the habit of grinding their own wheat flour form the local wheat mills. At present two a tune of about 4 TMT of soy flour is going in this market. In addition to mixing of soy flour to wheat flour, significant number of households especially in north India buys whole beans from local markets to grind with wheat. This use of whole soybean in this sector is almost to a tune of 40-45 TMT.

Gram Soy Flour

Is another potential area, which can move soy off-take quickly. This is relatively new area and we started working only in 2001.

Soymilk and Tofu

Soymilk is gaining popularity in India especially in the last two years. In spite of past failures

Future

Soymilk

In the next few years, a conservative estimate puts the soymilk consumption almost at 1 MMT with a potential for beans of 273 TMT. This growth will be just from a mere 63 MT in FY 00. This particular segment has a great scope for importing the U.S. soybeans directly if the SPS issues are resolved. In FY02 we have already seen interest in importing the beans mainly because the soybean quality in the last four months of year has gone down and prices shoot up drastically. If we add the potential in the whole region, there is much higher scope for soymilk production and greater demand for the U.S. beans as the other countries in the region has very limited scope for production of soymilk.

Table 26.1

Year	Soymilk Production (MT)	Soybean Utilization (MT)	Sales (lac Rs)	Sales (Mil$)
99–00*	442.8	63.3	221.4	0.46
00–01*	1,154.0	164.8	576.9	1.20
01–02*	3,655.8	457.0	1827.9	3.79
02–03	10,243.8	1,455.7	5121.9	10.63
03–04	29,194	4,148.7	14597.4	30.3
04–05	83,205	11,824	41602.6	86.3
05–06	23,7135	33,698	118568	246
06–07	67,5834	96,040	337917	701
07–08	1,926,129	273,713	963065	1999

*: Actual figures

Table 26.2

Year	Flour	TVP	Soy-milk and Tofu	Bake-ry	Health Suppl (ISP)	Whole	ICDS	Nood-les	Nuts	Total
2000	0.875	75	0.07	13	15.75	20	28.75	-	-	153
2001	1.875	100	0.16	15	35	30	31.25	-	-	213
2002	3.125	119	0.50	19	21	50	37.5	1.25	0.01	251
2003	12.5	150	2.00	30	28	70	46.25	6.25	0.50	346
2004	25	188	10.00	39	52.5	90	57.5	18.75	1.00	481
2005	37.5	225	30.00	50	105	100	72.5	37.5	2.00	660
2006	62.5	275	80.00	66	175	120	90	50	4.00	923
2007	100	313	120.00	80	262.5	130	112.5	68.75	10.00	1196
2008	137.5	375	150.00	100	350	150	137.5	93.75	20.00	1514

Flour: Wheat and gram flours

Health supplements are isolates

ICDS: Feeding programs

Figures are given as Soybean Equivalent (SBE)

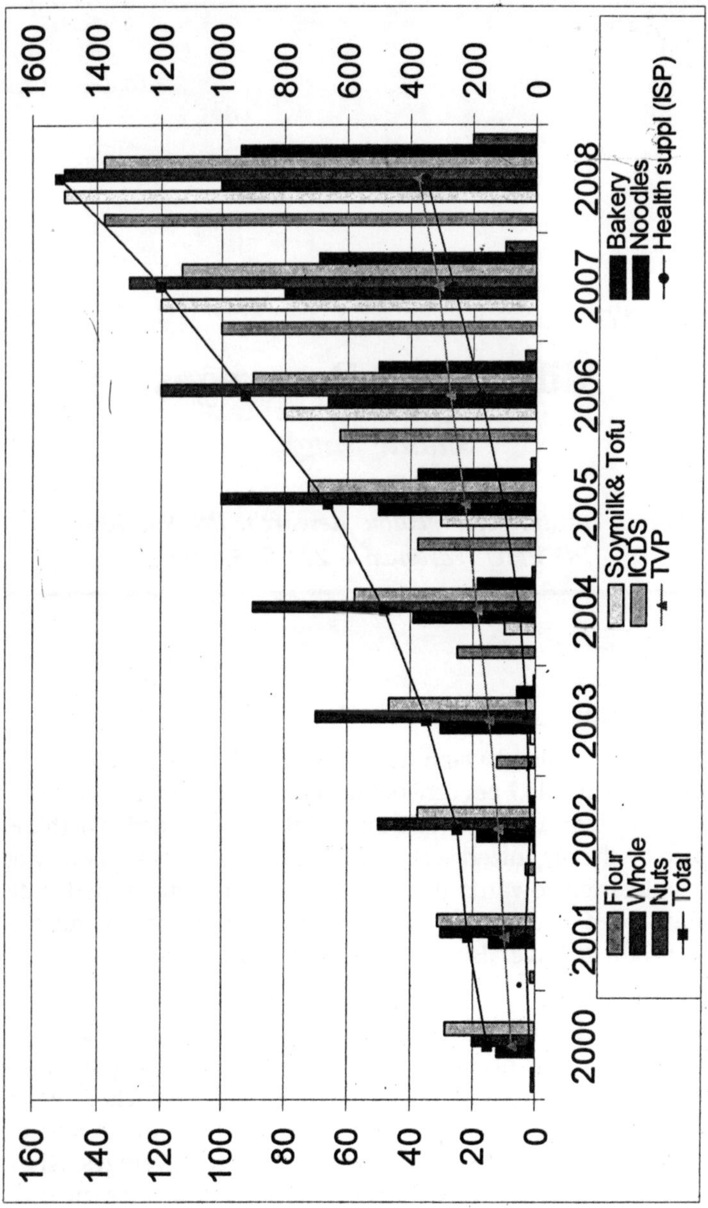

Figure 26.1: Soybean (SBE) Off-Take in India

Chapter 27

Milk Based Beverages

Sudhir Singh
Sr. Scientist
Indian Institute of Vegetable Research, PB No. 5002, PO BHU, Varanasi – 221 005, U.P.

Introduction

India has attained a significant position in milk production in the world. Nearly 45.7 per cent of the total milk produced in India is believed to be consumed as fluid milk. Only a small fraction of this is handled by the organized sector of the industry. Large quantity of milk is diverted towards the manufacture of value added milk products such as cheese, paneer, channa, casein, shrikhand etc. These products have also gained popularity in the international market.

Milk based flavoured milk is an integral part in all milk plants as these flavoured milks have good consumer acceptance as refreshing and nourishing milk beverages and also acts as great sales builder. These milks have good demand in the urban masses especially in the children. Apart from milk based beverages, whey utilization has been of great concern in the dairy industries engaged in the manufacture of cheese and coagulated milk products.

Flavoured Milk

Flavoured milk is defined as cow or buffalow milk or any of the designated milks such as single toned, double toned, recombined or standardized milk to which flavour either natural or synthetic flavour has been added. Sugar and colour may or may not be added depending on the requirements. If the flavoured milk is prepared from such milk which does not conform to any minimum legal standards in respect to fat and SNF, it is termed as flavoured drink or flavoured dairy drinks. The flavoured milks and flavoured drinks may be either pasteurized or sterilized.

Artificially Flavoured Milks

An artificial flavour is added for manufacturing these flavoured milks. The fat in milk is adjusted to about 2 per cent but SNF content is increased upto 10 per cent by the addition of reconstituted skim milk powder or butter milk powder. Standardized milk is homogenized at 65°C by two stage process. Homogenization is an inevitable step while manufacturing sterilized flavoured milk but could be eliminated in the preparation of pasteurized flavoured milk. The sugar @ 6 – 8 per cent is mixed properly with hot milk followed by pasteurization at 71°C for 30 min or 80°C for 15 sec and cooling to about 4°C. Finally, desired desired flavour 21 ml/kg milk is added at this stage. For the preparation of sterilized, flavoured milk, flavour @1.5 – 2.0 ml/kg of milk should be added before sterilization. A suitable thickener such as sodium alginate, carrageenan or CMC (upto 0.2 per cent) may also be added for improving the consistency in flavoured milks. Partial or complete replacement of sucrose with corn syrup has also been recommended. Flavoured milks could also be enriched with milk proteins, vitamins and minerals. Various types of artificial flavours such as vanilla, banana, pineaaple, rose, raspberry, strawberry, mango, orange, etc. are available in market. The choice of flavour should depend on consumers acceptance. In certain parts of India cardamom is used as as a natural flavouring material in the preparation of sterilized flavoured milk.

Chocolate Flavored Milk

Chocolate milk is most liked flavoured milk in most of the countries. Different types of chocolate milk is prepared depending upon its composition and the availability of raw materials used.

The different trends in utilization of different ingredients for ite preparation imvolve:

1. Normally low fat milk (Fat content ranging from 2.0 – 3.5 per cent) is preferred for chocolate milk preparation. However, skimmed milk may also be used. The milk SNF content is normally adjusted to 9 per cent or above.
2. Cocoa is most widely used as a flavouring material @ 1-1.5 per cent but liquor chocolate (1.5 – 2.0 per cent) which is considered to have a better flavour, can also be used although there are stability difficulties. Chocolate syrups may also be prepared in dairy plants by blending cocoa, sugar and stabilizer in desired proportions.
3. Sucrose @ 5-8 per cent is commonly used as the source of sweetness. This can however, be partially replaced by dextrose. Sucrose is now also replaced by high fructose corn syrup (HFCS) in chocolate milk because HFCS has a lesser

Chapter 28

Shelf Life Studies on Indian Milk Products

Sudhir Singh
Sr. Scientist
Indian Institute of Vegetable Research, PB No. 5002, PO BHU, Varanasi – 221 005, U.P.

Introduction

India has emerged as largest milk producer in the world. Half of the milk produced in India is utilized as fluid milk and rest of milk is converted in to traditional indigenous dairy products. Furthermore, only 10-15 per cent of the total milk produced is processed by the organized dairy sector. A large proportion of milk is converted into Indian milk products such as ghee, paneer, chhana and khoa etc.

The indigenous milk products are mainly produced by small scale traders and halwais except for about 15 per cent of total ghee is contributed by the organized dairy sectors. The traditional methods are good for cottage scale which do not permit efficient utilization of fuel. These processes are labour intensive. The quality of Indian milk products varies in respect of moisture, texture and flavour. The quality of milk used, degree of heat treatment, manner of handling of products and duration and condition of storage lead to variations in the chemical composition which pose problems in the production of uniform quality sweets.

The unhygienic conditions at the production centres lead to contamination of products with different types of micro organisms leading to low shelf life of these products. The problem gets aggravated during summer month in respect of composition, microbial quality, sensory properties and shelf life. A variety of micro organisms comprising of mesophiles, acid producers, spore farmers, coliforms, staphylococci, yeast and mould, can be located in indigenous milk products.

Most of the indigenous milk products are sold in the market without proper packaging and unduly exposing to atmospheric contamination. It is thus, not feasible to lay down any microbiological standards for these products.

Shelf Life Studies of Indian Milk Products

Ghee

Ghee has a long shelf life to resist spoilage by elemental and microbial means than any other milk products. However, it is on common knowledge that upon prolonged storage at ambient temperature, it undergoes oxidative changes. Reaction of oxygen with unsaturated fat is a major cause of spoilage. It gives rise to a typical, strong and disagreeable odour. Production of off flavour results in the loss of nutritive value.

Auto oxidation of ghee is aggravated by metallic contamination and sunlight. The acceleration effect of light is dependent on its wave length and visible light accelerates the decomposition of hydroperoxidase. Ultraviolet light has more pronounced effect than the impact of other rays. High energy radiations such as β and γ rays exert a pronounced acceleration effect because the generation of hydroperodixase and free radicals is responsible for off flavour development from the molecules of unoxidized substrate.

The durability of ghee is affected by the degree of unsaturation of the fat, the temperature at which the ghee is stored, the manner in which the milk of ghee making was handled, uncontrolled fermentation during curdling, uneven heating during manufacture and insanitary conditions of the vessels used for the production and storage of ghee.

A number of synthetic antioxidants such as gallates (ethyl, propyl, octyl) butylated hydroxytoluene (BHT), butylated hydroxyanisole (BHA), tertiary butyl hydroquinons (TBHQ), ascorbic acid, α-tocopherol, phospholipids and some natural antioxidants, namely curry leaves, betel leaves, soybean powder, safflower and amla can be added in small amounts with a view to either complete prevention or partial retardation of fat during storage.

The antioxidative properties of curry and betel leaves can be attributed to their phenolic compounds, predominantly hydroxychavicol. The ascorbic acid enriched leaves may act synergistically. Curry leaves and betel leaves also contain many amino acid, which serve as antioxidants. The age old practice of boiling betel and curry leaves with desi butter at the time of clarification helps to improve the flavour, colour and shelf life of ghee.

Khoa

The average shelf life of khoa at 37±1°C, 23-24°C and 5-10°C is reported 7, 10 and 25 days, respectively. In the absence of proper packaging materials, the moisture loss from the product adversely affects the texture and enhances the rate of chemical deterioration such as oxidation and browning. The effect of packaging materials and preservatives have significant effect on the shelf life of khoa. The shelf life of khoa is increased to 13 days at 13°C and to 75 days in the cold storage during storage in the four ply laminated pouches and tin containers. Sterilization of polypacks with gamma radiation using CO^{60} prior to product filling proved to be beneficial. Addition of 0.3 per cent potassium sorbate during the last stage of khoa making increased the shelf life of khoa by another 10 days. Vacuum packing of khoa could enhance the shelf life upto 120 days during refrigerated storage.

The shelf life of khoa can be extended by converting khoa to khoa powder. Khoa is uniformly distributed on aluminium trays and is dried separately in vacuum and atmospheric hot oven at 70°C. The grated khoa is dried in fludized bed dryer with inlet temperature of 98°C. Khoa can be dried in 30 minutes in fluidized bed dryer. Khoa powder can also be developed by spray drying process. Concentrated milk with 30 per cent total solids is subjected to heat treatments to develop cooked flavour. The heated, concentrated milk is atomized and instantly dried in an Anhydrospray drier with an inlet temperature of 190°C and outlet temperature of 78°C. Khoa powder is cooled to room temperature and is packed in suitable packaging materials.

Khoa powder has a shelf life of 5-6 months at room temperature. Nitrogen gas flushing and addition of BHA further enhanced the shelf life to 11 months.

Paneer

The relatively short life of pancer is a major handicap on the commercial adoption of paneer manufacture. The shelf life of paneer is reported to be only 6 days under refrigerated condition though its freshness is lost within 3 days. At room temperature paneer is not stored for more than one day. The heat treatment to milk during the manufacture of paneer is more than enough to destroy all the pathogenic spoilage micro organisms. Post manufacturing contamination is responsible for the spoilage of paneer. The spoilage in paneer occurs due to the surface growth of micro organisms. A greenish yellow slime forms on the surface and the discolouration is accompanied by off flavour development during storage. The shelf life of paneer can be further increased by following methods:

Chilling

Rapid chilling of paneer is necessary to arrest the growth of micro organisms. It is necessary for the processor to reduce the paneer temperature to 5-10°C at the time of packaging. Good quality water should be used for chilling of paneer.

Brining

Paneer dipped in 5 per cent brine solution lasts for nearly 20 days as against control paneer is spoiled after 6 days of storage at 8-10°C. The sensory attributes are rated higher for salted samples. Since paneer is mostly salted and spiced before consumption, the salting at the time of dipping can be used in extending the shelf life of paneer.

Use of Chemical Preservatives

A shelf life of 32 days under refrigeration can be achieved when paneer is treated with a combination of delvocid and hydrogen peroxide. Shelf life of 40 days using benzoic acid (1200 ppm) under refrigerated conditions and 20 days at 37°C has been reported.

However, shelf life of 36 days at room temperature is achieved by adding sorbic acid to milk (0.15 per cent) and subsequent wrapping of paneer in sorbic acid coated paper.

Freezing

The flavour and appearance of paneer is not affected on frozen of paneer at –13°C and –32°C for 120 days. However, the body and texture deteriorates and the paneer becomes crumbly and fluffy upon thawing. Blast freezing has been used to enhance the shelf life of paneer. The paneer blocks cut into small size are blast frozen at a temperature below –20°C. Paneer can be stored for more than one year without any deterioration in the quality.

Vacuum Packaging

Vacuum packaging of paneer in laminated pouches can increase the shelf life of paneer to about 30 days at 6±1°C. The body and texture of paneer is also improved on vacuum packaging as it becomes more compact and shows better sliceability. Paneer packaged in cryovac vacuum packaging and heat treated at 90°C for one minute can maintain the shelf life of paneer of 90 days at refrigeration temperature.

Heat Sterilization of Paneer

The shelf life of paneer is markedly improved at refrigeration temperature. However, the shelf life of paneer is not improved noticeably. Heat sterilization of paneer is an effective treatment for improving the shelf life of paneer at room temperature. Paneer packed in tins along with water/brine and sterilization at 15 psi for 15 minutes can extend the shelf life of paneer to 4 months.

Microwave Drying of Hot Diffused Paneer

Hot diffusion (60°C for 5 minutes in 2.5 per cent sodium chloride and 0.5 per cent potassium sorbate) and cold diffusion (5-10 °C for 6 hours in 2.5 per cent sodium chloride and 0.5 per cent potassium sorbate) process in paneer and subsequent microwave drying (80 per cent power level for 5 minutes) and vacuum packaging is reported to extend the shelf life to 90 days under refrigerated storage. The dried paneer has no fat loss and apparent browning and is rehydrated well at 30°C for 10 minutes.

Hurdle Technology Concept for Preservation of Paneer

The shelf life in paneer is achieved by inactivation of micro organisms. The shelf life extension in paneer is achieved by inherent preservation factors such as extent of heat treatment, water activity, low temperature storage, redox potential, pH etc. These preservative factors act as hurdles because micro organisms would have to jump these hurdles in order to grow and spoil the product. The stability of paneer depends upon the intensity of hurdles present in it. In conventional preservation method, the intensity of one or two of these hurdles is exceptionally increased making it extremely difficult for micro organisms to jump that hurdle. Paneer can be preserved for a long time by heat treatment alone, but there is immense damage to texture and nutritive value. Paneer's keeping quality can also be considerably extended by dehydration process. However the reconstituability of paneer is poor and the texture is adversely affected. However, by using three or more hurdles together, the damage to sensory properties is not only kept minimum but also their synergistic action is exploited for paneer preservation. In hurdle technology, every preservative parameter is kept at optimum level in order to get maximum microbial inactivation by combination of two or more such parameters so that damage to the sensory properties of food is kept to the minimum level.

Shrikhand

Shrikhand, an acid coagulated sweetened milk product is popular in Gujarat, Maharashtra and Karnataka. Shrikhand has fairly long shelf life of 35-40 days at 8°C and 2-3 days at 30°C. The keeping quality depends largely on the initial level of contaminating organisms particularly yeast and moulds. The keeping quality is seriously affected by proteolytic microflora under refrigerated conditions of storage. The spoiled shrikhand samples exhibit off flavours like fruiting, fermented and rancid along with surface discolouration. Addition of 0.5 per cent potassium sorbate prevents the growth of yeast and moulds. Heating of shrikhand at 70°C for 2 minutes further improves the keeping quality of shrikhand.

Conclusion

The need for increasing the shelf life of indigenous dairy products is greatly realized for effective upgrading the technology for production on large scale. Newer innovations have helped in increasing the shelf life of indigenous dairy products considerably. The judicious use of permitted additives is desired for the safety of consumers.

References

Rajorhia, G.S. and Sherbon, J.W. (1986). Effect of processing conditions on the melting properties of ghee. Indian Dairyman 38(8), 381.

Rajorhia, G.S. (1998). Recent advances in the manufacture of Khoa. Centre of Advanced Studies in Dairy Technology, NDRI, Karnal.

Sachdeva, S. and Singh, S. (1990). Shelf life of paneer as affected by antimicrobial agents Part I. Effect on sensory characteristics. Ind. J. Dairy Sci. 43(1): 60.

Rao, K.J. (1993). Application of hundle technology in the development of long life paneer based convenience food. Ph.D. Thesis. NDRI Deemed University, Karnal.

Upadhyay, K.G. and Dave, J.M. (1977). Shrikhand and its technology. Indian Dairyman. 28(9): 487.

Index

R

S

T